M

Misguided Virtue

False Notions of Corporate Social Responsibility

DAVID HENDERSON

The Institute of Economic Affairs

First published in Great Britain in 2001 by
The Institute of Economic Affairs
2 Lord North Street
Westminster
London SW1P 3LB
in association with Profile Books Ltd

A CIP catalogue record for this book is available from the British Library.

ISBN 0 255 36510 1

Many IEA publications are translated into languages other than English or are reprinted. Permission to translate or to reprint should be sought from the General Director at the address above.

Typeset in Stone by MacGuru
info@macguru.org.uk

Printed and bound in Great Britain by Hobbs the Printers Ltd

CONTENTS

THE AUTHOR

David Henderson was formerly (1984–92) Head of the Economics and Statistics Department of the Organisation for Economic Cooperation and Development (the OECD) in Paris. Before that he had worked as an academic economist in Britain, first in Oxford (Fellow of Lincoln College) and later in University College London (Professor of Economics), as a British civil servant (first as an Economic Adviser in HM Treasury, and later as Chief Economist in the UK Ministry of Aviation), and as a staff member of the World Bank. In 1985 he gave the BBC Reith Lectures, which were published in book form under the title *Innocence and Design: The Influence of Economic Ideas on Policy* (Blackwell, 1986).

Since leaving the OECD he has been an independent author and consultant, and has acted as Visiting Fellow or Professor at the OECD Development Centre (Paris), the Centre for European Policy Studies (Brussels), Monash University (Melbourne), the Fondation Nationale des Sciences Politiques (Paris), the University of Melbourne, the Royal Institute of International Affairs (London), the New Zealand Business Roundtable, and the Melbourne Business School. He is currently Visiting Professor at the Westminster Business School. Among his recent publications is *The Changing Fortunes of Economic Liberalism* (IEA, London, 1998, and Melbourne, 1999; reissued in London with a new preface, 2001). He is an Honorary Fellow of Lincoln College, Oxford, and in 1992 he was made Commander of the Order of St Michael and St George.

FOREWORD

SHAREHOLDER VALUE AND CORPORATE SOCIAL RESPONSIBILITY

Since World War II Western capitalism has passed through two distinct phases. The first was managerial capitalism. During the 1950s and 1960s directors of large corporations enjoyed a high degree of discretion in deciding how to use the resources at their disposal, what new businesses to enter, how much to spend on scientific research. Except in cases of egregious mismanagement, shareholders were generally passive. These comfortable conditions gave way in the 1970s, and more decisively in the 1980s and 1990s, to a new phase which came to be known as investor capitalism. Chief executives and boards of directors found themselves under growing pressure from a new breed of activist investor and from a more highly developed market for corporate control. Companies which failed to maximise shareholder value were likely to face demands for changes in management, or a hostile takeover bid.

Are we now entering a third phase, which might be called socially responsible capitalism? One of the central themes in David Henderson's paper is the emergence of a new way of thinking about the functions and duties of the modern corporation. This approach, which is rapidly acquiring the status of conventional wisdom, puts much less weight on the sovereignty of shareholders and much more on the responsibility of corporate managers to serve the needs of society at large. It is a philosophy which unites not only non-governmental organisations and some governments, but a growing number of leading private-sector managers. They are serviced by an army of consultants and academics who specialise in teaching and advising on such fashionable subjects as 'triple bottom line reporting' – a form of reporting which gives equal prominence to the financial, environmental and social aspects of a company's performance.

The argument to which all these groups subscribe is that making profits for shareholders has to be tempered by a range of other considerations; these include a responsibility to protect the environment and to contribute to the wellbeing of society. Some advocates of the new approach argue that these wider responsibilities should be enshrined in law. Others believe that the necessary changes can be brought about by self-regulation, codes of conduct and peer pressure.

How important is this line of thinking, and does it imply a radical departure from the focus on shareholder value which has been the dominant corporate ideology in the US and the UK for the past 20 years, and which is now spreading to other countries?

In answering these questions it is important to be clear about what caused the shift from managerial to investor capitalism, and about the consequences of that shift, not just for the way companies were run, but for economic performance.

For many, though not all, industries the first 30 years after the war were a golden age of rising demand, generous profit margins, and limited competitive pressure. A not untypical case was that of the US motor industry. The bulk of the market was in the hands of three companies, General Motors, Ford and Chrysler, and competition from imports was minimal. In these circumstances keeping investors happy was not difficult, and shareholder preferences did not loom large in the thinking of boards of directors. Corporate leaders tended to equate the interests of their companies with those of society as a whole. As the chairman of Standard Oil Company of New Jersey remarked, managers of his company aimed to 'maintain an equitable and working balance among the claims of the various directly interested groups – stockholders, employees, customers and the public at large'.

In the absence of critical scrutiny from the capital markets, managerial empire-building was rife, and this often took the form of investments, whether in new plant or in acquisitions of other companies, which yielded little return to investors. For a company such as Imperial Chemical Industries (ICI), which was the dominant player in the British chemical market, the driving force was technocratic rather than commercial; building a bigger ethylene cracker seemed a higher priority than making more money for shareholders.

The 1970s changed all that. A combination of factors, including the slowdown in the world economy after the 1973 oil crisis and the increase in exports from Japan and the newly industrialising countries, led to an erosion of profit margins. Competition intensified during the 1980s and 1990s as the trend towards liberalisation and deregulation, led by the Thatcher government in Britain, gathered pace. The stable oligopolies of the earlier postwar decades began to break up.

At the same time important changes were taking place in the capital markets. Ownership of publicly quoted companies was increasingly concentrated in the hands of large financial institutions, some of which adopted a more aggressive stance towards underperforming managements. There was also a wider range of sources of finance for smaller firms which were seeking to challenge the incumbents. Large size was no longer a defence against takeover.

Companies were forced to concentrate on businesses which were capable of competing in an open world market, and to withdraw from those which were not. A wave of closures and divestments transformed the structure of several industries. A notable example was the break-up of ICI in 1993, following a threatened takeover from Hanson. The demerging of ICI's pharmaceutical division into a separately quoted company (Zeneca) was designed to increase shareholder value. Some British commentators deplored what they saw as a panicky response to a threatened takeover bid. This, they said, was Anglo-American short-termism at its worst – it would never happen in Germany. Yet a few years later one of ICI's German competitors, Hoechst, adopted an even more radical approach, turning itself into a pure life sciences company (now called Aventis), and selling off all its traditional chemical businesses. Although Hoechst was not facing a threat of takeover, its strategy was dictated in large measure by the need to improve returns to shareholders. Since then the shareholder value movement in Germany has been gaining in influence.

Although the restructuring process was painful, it produced substantial economic benefits. Companies were deterred from making wasteful investments, and capital flowed into activities where it could earn a high return. Boards of directors were shaken out of their somnolence, recognising that their primary duty was to ensure that the company was run in the interests of shareholders; the sacking of the chief executive of General Motors in 1992 was a celebrated example.

The shift to investor capitalism has been facilitated, and to some extent positively encouraged, by governments. The trend in public policy, even in countries where parties of the left or centre-left are in power, has been to allow markets, including capital markets, freer rein. But this does not mean that investor capitalism is universally popular. On the contrary, many people believe that for companies to focus exclusively on shareholder value is both morally wrong and socially damaging.

According to this view, the activities of companies – especially large, multinational companies – impinge in a variety of ways on the health of the societies in which they operate, and on the environment. In return for the freedom which they enjoy in pursuing their commercial objectives, companies must recognise these externalities and adjust their behaviour accordingly.

How justified are these demands, and how should companies respond to them? Answers to these questions have to start from a clear understanding of what corporate social responsibility, as defined by its most influential proponents, really means. Yet, as David Henderson shows in this paper, precise definitions are hard to come by. An important ingredient, much emphasised by some non-governmental organisations, is a commitment on the part of companies to sustainable development. This is an appealing formula but, as Henderson points out, there is a great deal of uncertainty about what it means and about what it implies in practice for corporate behaviour. This is just one example of the woolly thinking which characterises much of the discussion on this subject.

It is also important to remember that many leading advocates of these ideas have little understanding of, and in some cases a deep distaste for, the capitalist system. Their interest is not in making the system work better, but in altering it in a way which suits their idea of what companies are for. Partly for this reason, too much of the debate has been distorted by half-truths and false assertions.

David Henderson's carefully argued critique will force all the participants in the debate to question their assumptions – not least those private-sector organisations which, whether influenced by political correctness or by the desire for a quiet life, have broadly gone along with the current fashion. This timely and important paper should encourage fresh thinking on the role which companies should play in a democratic, market-based society.

SIR GEOFFREY OWEN

Senior Fellow

Institute of Management

London School of Economics

July 2001

ACKNOWLEDGEMENTS

Work on this essay has extended over a long period, during which I was connected with five institutions: the Melbourne Business School, of which Professor John Rose was then Director; the New Zealand Business Roundtable, of which Roger Kerr is Executive Director; the Groupe d'Economie Mondiale, directed by Professor Patrick Messerlin at the Ecole Nationale des Sciences Politiques in Paris; the Institute of Economic Affairs in London, of which John Blundell is Director; and the Westminster Business School, of which Professor J. R. Shackleton is Dean. Thanks are due to all of these for the facilities and encouragement they provided, and to the New Zealand Business Roundtable for financial support. Helpful information, ideas, advice or comments came at different stages from Robin Aram, Sir Samuel Brittan, Tom Delfgaauw, Deniz Eröcal, Roger Kerr, Brink Lindsey, Patrick Messerlin, Guy Pfeffermann, Colin Robinson, John Rose, Ronald Steenblik, Benn Steil, Bryce Wilkinson, Philip Williams and Andrew Wilson, and I am grateful to them all. However, the responsibility for the way in which the issues are treated here, as also for the opinions expressed and conclusions drawn, is mine alone.

An earlier version of this paper was published in June 2001 by the New Zealand Business Roundtable.

SUMMARY

- While issues concerning the social responsibilities of businesses have long been the subject of debate, today's conception of Corporate Social Responsibility (CSR) marks a new departure.
- CSR assigns to businesses a new role and purpose. They are to embrace 'corporate citizenship', and run their affairs, in close conjunction with an array of different 'stakeholders', so as to promote the goal of 'sustainable development'. This goal supposedly has three dimensions, 'economic', 'environmental' and 'social'. Hence businesses should set objectives, measure their performance, and have that performance independently audited, in relation to all three. They should aim to meet the 'triple bottom line', rather than focusing on profitability and shareholder value.
- CSR holds that only by acting in such a way can businesses meet 'society's expectations', and earn from 'society' their informal 'licence to operate'. Hence a commitment to corporate citizenship is the key to long-run profitability for individual firms, and to ensuring public support for the market economy. Capitalism has to be given 'a human face'.
- CSR has caught on. It has been endorsed by a substantial and growing number of businesses, especially multinational

enterprises (MNEs); by business organisations; by academics and commentators; by so-called 'public interest' non-governmental organisations (NGOs); by investment institutions which stand for 'socially responsible investment'; by a growing army of advisers and consultants; by a range of international agencies; by the European Commission, in a recently-issued Green Paper; and by many governments. It has few overt critics.

- CSR supporters presume that the notion of sustainable development, and the actions needed to promote it, are well defined and generally agreed. This is not so.
- The notion of 'society's expectations' is open to question. Many supporters of CSR simply assume that these expectations are represented by what the critics of business among the NGOs are saying. But it is doubtful whether what most people now expect of businesses is that they should work with 'stakeholders' in pursuit of sustainable development and the 'triple bottom line'.
- Many advocates of CSR show a lack of understanding of the rationale of a market economy and the role of profits within it.
- Among CSR advocates, both in the business world and outside, there is wide support for *global salvationism*. This goes with acceptance of alarmist views on the state of the environment and the damage done to it by business-related activities, a belief that fateful choices now have to be made on behalf of humanity and the planet, and a distorted view of globalisation and its effects.
- Contrary to salvationist assumptions, it is not the case that globalisation has 'marginalised' or 'excluded' poor people or poor countries. It has not brought benefits to multinational

enterprises in particular, nor has it increased their power to influence events while weakening that of governments.

- Within businesses, the adoption of CSR carries with it a high probability of cost increases and impaired performance. Managers have to take account of a wider range of goals and concerns, and involve themselves in new processes of consultation with 'stakeholders'. New systems of accounting, monitoring and auditing are called for. On top of all this, the adoption of more exacting self-chosen environmental and 'social' standards is liable to add to costs – all the more so if, as is required by CSR, firms insist on observance of these same standards by their partners, suppliers and contractors.

- CSR embodies the notion that progress in relation to environmental and social issues lies in making norms and standards more stringent and more uniform, in part by corporations acting on their own initiative. This approach takes too little account of costs and benefits at the margin, and of differences in circumstances which may bear on these. It points the way to extending regulation in ways that would reduce welfare. The effects of enforced uniformity are especially damaging in labour markets.

- The greatest potential for harm of this kind arises from attempts, whether by governments or by businesses in the name of CSR and 'global corporate citizenship', to regulate the world as a whole. Imposing common international standards, despite the fact that circumstances may be widely different across countries, restricts the scope for mutually beneficial trade and investment flows. It is liable to hold back the development of poor countries through the suppression of employment opportunities within them.

- In so far as 'socially responsible' businesses find that their new role is bringing with it higher costs and lower profits, they have a strong interest in having their unregenerate rivals compelled to follow suit, whether through public pressure or government regulation. The effect of such enforced uniformity is to limit competition and hence to worsen the performance of the economy as a whole. The system effects of CSR, as well as the enterprise effects, will tend to make people in general poorer.

- Businesses and business organisations that support CSR have typically failed to contest, or have even endorsed, the arguments and demands of anti-business activist groups. Their strategy is one of appeasement and accommodation. They show little awareness that the case for private business derives from its links with competition and economic freedom. They mistakenly identify defence of the market economy with making businesses more popular and respected, through meeting 'society's expectations'. Whether all this is responsible conduct is open to doubt.

- With few exceptions, the contribution of the business world to public debate on these broad issues of public policy has been, and continues to be, inadequate or worse. It is time for some leading corporations to consider how they could improve this state of affairs.

- CSR rests on a mistaken view of issues and events, and its general adoption by businesses would reduce welfare and undermine the market economy.

1 THE CHALLENGE OF CSR

The subject of this paper, which is as old as capitalism itself, is that of rules for the proper conduct of business enterprises. Issues concerning the rationale, performance and behaviour of privately owned business corporations have a long history of inquiry and debate. While this has chiefly involved the three overlapping areas of business ethics, corporate governance and company law, the subject can also be treated, as here, in the context of the economics of public policy. Whatever the approach, two central and inter-related questions arise. The first is that of the legal obligations to which businesses should be made subject. The second concerns the responsibilities that businesses should recognise and live up to, over and above those that are imposed on them by law.

This latter aspect has itself a long history; and for some decades at any rate, it has often been discussed in terms of defining and interpreting 'corporate social responsibility'. But in recent years, in response to developments on the world scene, a recognisably new approach has emerged and caught on. A well-worn concept has been reinterpreted and given new life. A growing number of major companies, with widespread and increasing support from outside the business world, have now embraced, and are actively promoting, the present-day conception of Corporate Social Responsibility (CSR) which is the particular focus of this paper. Hence there are two conceptions or doctrines to be distinguished.

One is the general notion of corporate social responsibility, which is not new and is mentioned here only in passing. The other is the specific modern development of it which I review below. In what follows, the shorthand description of 'CSR' is reserved for this alone.

CSR raises twin issues that lie at the heart of the economics of public policy. One is whether and how far the self-interested actions of individual economic agents in a market economy, including in particular the actions of business enterprises guided by the profit motive, will further the common good. The second concerns what can be done, whether by people and enterprises on their own account or through action by governments, to ensure that private and public interests are brought more closely into line, and in particular, to make enterprise profitability a better indicator of social welfare.

In its treatment of these leading issues, CSR makes far-reaching proposals. It assigns a central role to corporations themselves, arguing for a new and wider conception of what private business stands for and how it should be conducted. In taking this line, it parts company from the teachings of standard economics – though in both camps there are various shades of opinion, so that the generalisation is a broad one only.

Characteristically though far from unanimously, those economists who have concerned themselves with the general notion of corporate social responsibility have been lukewarm or hostile towards it. In part, this is because of a belief that businesses will be less efficiently run in so far as managers set themselves goals other than profitability. A second concern, which might be termed constitutional, is that businesses have no right to define such goals. This point of view was memorably stated, almost four decades ago, by Milton Friedman in *Capitalism and Freedom*:

> Few trends could so thoroughly undermine the very
> foundations of our free society as the acceptance by
> corporate officials of a social responsibility other than to
> make as much money for their stockholders as possible.
> This is a fundamentally subversive doctrine. If businessmen
> do have a social responsibility other than making maximum
> profits for stockholders, how are they to know what it is?
> Can self-selected private individuals decide what the social
> interest is? (p. 133).

The particular economic approach thus set out does not advocate unqualified laissez-faire. Rather, it reserves to governments the responsibility for deciding both where the public interest lies and what measures would help to ensure that profit-maximising businesses will serve it.

In effect, there is an alliance here between mainstream economics and traditional doctrines of corporate governance. The economists referred to view profitability as a prima facie indicator of changes in general welfare: this is their starting point. Hence they want firms to maximise profits. Since the profits accrue to shareholders, and these are presumed to want to maximise their gains, it follows that the managers of firms should act in the interests of shareholders. By contrast, the starting point of traditional views of corporate governance is that firms have a fiduciary duty to act in accordance with the interests of their owners, the shareholders. In so far as these interests are defined in terms of the returns to shareholders, however, this becomes a duty to maximise profits. Though their initial premises are different, the conclusions of the two groups are much the same. Since both give pre-eminence to shareholders, they are cool towards the idea, now widely accepted, that power or status should be conferred, whether by law or corporate decisions, on other 'stakeholders' in a business. Both believe that companies will best discharge the responsibilities which specifically belong to them by taking profitability as a guide, subject always to acting within the law, and that they should not go out of their way to define and promote wider self-chosen objectives.

Contrary to what is sometimes maintained, this common traditionalist approach does not at all rule out the exercise of independent moral judgements by those involved in business activities. Clearly, there are many situations in which managers, and indeed shareholders too, may need to consider what it would be right to do as well as what is both legal and profitable. Sir Samuel Brittan has used as an illustration (Brittan, 1989: 5) that 'The absence of effective legislation should not excuse a chemical company for polluting the air.' Both shareholders and boards of directors may be willing, and arguably should be willing, to risk or forgo profits at the margin for such causes as ensuring product safety, disclosing possible safety risks, reducing harmful pollution, eschewing bribery, or dealing fairly with other parties, even where no legal obligations are in question. Such exceptions, and cases where there are good grounds for exercising independent judgement, are liable to arise even in countries that have well-functioning legal systems and governments: laws and official regulations may lag behind events, and in any case cannot be expected to cover all contingencies. Where governments are corrupt, authoritarian or ineffective, the range of debatable issues and problems, and the need for companies to make their own assessments and judgements, become greater. Everywhere there may be episodes and situations where the issue of what constitutes responsible conduct on the part of a business has to be faced, and cannot be left to governments alone to review, decide and pronounce on.

These considerations, however, are not new. They qualify but do not invalidate the general case for treating profitability, and the interests of shareholders, as the primary concern and objective of privately owned businesses, and for taking a restricted view of both the right and the competence of a business to go beyond this. This traditionalist view of the responsibilities of companies remains influential, nor has it been driven from the field by the advent of CSR. Those who hold to it believe that the primary role and due pretensions of companies have not changed with the times.

By contrast, the CSR approach is in large part a response to recent developments, or what are perceived as such. It maintains that a new and broader conception of the social responsibilities of business is now called for everywhere, because of the ways in which the world has changed. Businesses are seen as having to respond to new demands, new challenges, and new opportunities and possibilities for action. In this situation (the argument goes), it is not sufficient for them to think exclusively, or even primarily, in terms of profitability and the interests of owners. To do so would in fact be self-defeating: it would go against the true long-run interests of shareholders themselves, and could well put in doubt the future of capitalism and the market economy. Businesses today should make explicit commitments to uphold accepted values and goals, and to take account of the views and interests of a range of stakeholders; and they should demonstrate through their actions that these commitments are genuine. That such a prescription may hold attractions for economists as well as others is indicated by the announcement (*Financial Times*, 7 February 2001) that in Britain a 'new network for socially responsible business, GoodCorporation', would be chaired by the chief economic adviser to KPMG, a leading accounting and consulting firm. The GoodCorporation website now shows messages of support, and two of these come from leading economists in Britain. One of the duo is Meghnad Desai, who is a professor of economics at the London School of Economics and a member of the House of Lords. Lord Desai's endorsement begins:

> Business has a key role to play in the global community. By demonstrating commitment to all stakeholders through responsible and ethical behaviour businesses can begin to fulfil this role.

This is a far cry from the traditionalist view of corporate responsibilities.

Evidence that this new alternative way of thinking has caught on, and of what it may imply for the orientation and conduct of businesses, will be presented below: I build up by stages a portrait of CSR. A preliminary glimpse of what is involved can be caught from some of the 'mission statements' which many big companies have now chosen to adopt. While these vary a good deal, they typically specify a range of goals and aspirations going well beyond profitability and returns to shareholders. Two prominent multinational enterprises (MNEs), ABB and Rio Tinto, can be taken as illustrations: like many other companies, they provide mission statements on their websites. A key paragraph in *A Brief Guide to ABB* reads as follows:

> ABB's vision is to create value. We create value for our customers by making them more competitive. For our employees, by offering them opportunities to learn, grow and share in the value that they create. We manage for value to meet or exceed the expectations of our shareholders. For the communities where we operate and for society at large, we create value by living our commitment to sustainable development.

Again, the second paragraph of a Rio Tinto statement entitled *The way we work* reads:

> Rio Tinto aims to develop the world's mineral resources in a responsible manner for the long-term benefit of its shareholders, employees, customers and the countries in which those resources are located.

Admittedly, the significance of such official pronouncements, and indeed of the whole recent trend towards CSR, is open to doubt. How far the new language, attitudes and outlook represent a true innovation, rather than a mere repackaging of old ideas with some effective marketing behind it, is a matter of opinion – the more so since what is involved is still in course of being defined and given shape. Again, while the issues that CSR addresses are general, its architects and advocates within the business community typically come from the large MNEs, whose interests are international or even worldwide. There is a question as to how far its precepts, even if they may hold good for these companies, are applicable to small and medium-sized firms whose public profile is lower and whose concerns are more local. Even for the leading corporations that have subscribed to the doctrine there may be, in some cases at any rate, room for doubt as to whether much more is really involved than well-publicised window-dressing. It is possible that this whole recent development will prove to be little more than a passing fashion, largely confined to the big multinationals and with no serious or lasting impact even on them.

On present evidence, however, this is not the most likely outcome. The way of thinking that enters into CSR, and the growing, broadly based and influential support for it both among businesses and more generally, deserve to be taken seriously for several reasons.

First, it is not only the large firms that are or may become involved. Much of the doctrine applies generally, and most enterprises of any size could find themselves encouraged, or brought under pressure, to embrace it in part or in full. Two governments that have given formal approval to the general notion of corporate social responsibility, in Denmark and the United Kingdom, have explicitly done so in the context of their business communities as a whole, including small and medium-sized enterprises; and as will be seen, firms in this latter group may increasingly be drawn in at the insistence of MNEs. One element in CSR is an obligation on its practitioners to do their best to ensure that other firms conform to it.

Second, CSR has to be set in a wider context. The ideas that enter into it do not comprise an isolated or self-contained system. They form part of a broader and highly influential current of opinion, extending well beyond the domain of business, which offers a perspective on present-day world developments and the questions of policy that they are seen as raising. This approach to current economic and political issues may be termed *global salvationism*. It comprises both a critique of the market-oriented economic systems of today and a programme of global reform which typically includes, as a leading element, the general adoption of CSR by businesses.

Third, and as will be further documented, CSR is a radical doctrine, both in what it says and in the consequences that it is liable to bring about. If it were generally adopted and put into effect, this could have profound implications for the conduct of business enterprises, and for the working and performance of economic systems. The possible effects are not confined within national boundaries: they extend to international trade and investment, the economic prospects of developing countries, and even the conduct of politics.

Thus CSR presents a challenge to what is still prevailing thought and practice, and its emergence may well be significant. There is good reason to consider just what enters into it, and what might be the consequences if it continues to spread and take root. That is what this essay seeks to do. Hence its scope is limited. I do not put forward a considered view as to how corporate social responsibilities are best defined in the world of today. Again, I do not seek to defend traditionalist ideas as such, nor to imply that these represent the only alternative to CSR. Rather, I outline the doctrine of CSR itself, drawing extensively on what its supporters have said and written, and offer a critique of it. I give reasons for thinking that it rests on a mistaken view of issues and events, and that its general adoption would reduce welfare and undermine the market economy.

The argument that follows is in six parts. Part 2 comprises summary history. It lists some recent influences which have persuaded many large businesses to re-examine their role and conduct, describes how the notion of CSR has emerged from this process, and notes its spread and growing acceptance both in the business world and outside. In Parts 3 to 5, the focus is mainly on ideas. Part 3 outlines the content and main distinctive features of the doctrine, drawing on reports and public statements from some of its leading business advocates. It concludes that supporters of CSR presume a consensus which is more apparent than real, and that the changes that it implies for businesses are far reaching and go beyond past notions of corporate social responsibility. Part 4 reviews the implications of CSR for the conduct and profitability of individual companies. I make the point that, while supporters generally state their case in terms of profitability, so that endorsing the doctrine is presented as no more than enlightened corporate self-interest in the world of today, many of them believe in it for its own sake. What CSR points towards is a radical reinterpretation of the role of private business, a new model for capitalism. Part 5 goes beyond the business world, and sketches in the broader background. It outlines and comments on the widely held ideas of global salvationism, which provide much of the underlying support for CSR and a rationale for its vision of capitalism made anew. I give reasons for rejecting the picture of reality which global salvationism offers. Part 6 deals with the possible consequences of putting CSR into practice – for individual firms, economic systems as a whole, and international trade and investment. I argue that the effect would be to worsen economic performance and to make people in general worse off, the more so in so far as the actions of companies are complemented or taken farther by outside pressures, sanctions and regulations. I also comment on some worrying political presumptions and judgements that are linked to CSR. Part 7 offers a general perspective and a specific proposal for improving the contribution of business to public debate. Part 8 is an addition to the text as first published by the New Zealand Business Roundtable. In it I review the recently published European Commission Green Paper on CSR, respond to some comments on what I have written, and extend the argument as a whole.

2 THE RISE OF CSR

Over the decade of the 1990s, a number of interrelated and mutually reinforcing developments on the world scene have given a new dimension to the debate on the role and responsibilities of private business corporations. They have caused businesses generally, and the MNEs in particular, to review their aims, policies and ways of operating. CSR has emerged from this process.

Two of the influences that have been at work, neither of which is new, are:

- Continuing official and public concern with environmental issues and what are seen as threats to the environment, including in particular the possible risks arising from greenhouse gas emissions. Increasingly, this concern has found expression in the idea that actions and policies everywhere should be focused on the objective of *sustainable development*.
- Suspicion of, or hostility towards, MNEs, private business in general, profit-motivated behaviour, and the market economy.

Alongside these, four further related factors have emerged in recent years, namely:

- The development of stakeholder theories of business ethics and corporate governance.
- Globalisation, and its effects both real and (still more) supposed.
- The growing strength, influence and assertiveness of the NGOs. These are non-governmental organisations – hence the initials – but they are distinct from other organisations which are likewise non-governmental, such as groups representing businesses, professional groups or employees. They stand, not for particular sectional interests, but for causes. Hence they are often given the tactically useful label of 'public interest' groups. They include consumer associations, conservation and environmental groups, societies concerned with economic development in poor countries, human rights groups, movements for social justice, humanitarian societies, organisations representing indigenous peoples, and church groups from all denominations. They are often classed together, misleadingly, under the heading of 'civil society': this label also is tactically useful. Their effectiveness has now been much increased through the use of the Internet as a means of co-ordinating their activities across the world and reaching a wider audience. Although today's 'public interest' NGOs differ widely in their views and concerns, those of them that engage with economic issues, which make up the great majority, are with few exceptions suspicious of, or hostile to, private businesses generally and MNEs in particular.
- The shock effect of episodes in which leading companies were subject to well-publicised, hostile and damaging campaigns, with NGOs in the lead. Here some notable instances include the Royal Dutch/Shell Group in the mid-1990s, over the

Brent Spar episode and its operations in Nigeria; a number of businesses, including Reebok and Nike, over wages and working conditions in the plants of their overseas suppliers; and McDonald's, which has been accused, among other things, of deliberately encouraging forms of eating which are dangerous to health. In some cases, of which Shell was the most conspicuous, the firms involved suffered costly and even humiliating setbacks.

These more recent developments went with, and in part resulted from, a shift in attitudes. Public opinion, or at least some conspicuous elements within it, has grown more actively critical of business corporations. Businesses in general, and more especially the MNEs, have become subject to new forms of questioning, new demands, new pressures, and new expectations as to their aims and policies. More than ever, the sales, profitability and growth of a large international corporation appear now to depend on its reputation, on what people in general, including not only outsiders but also its own employees, think of its conduct. This is apt to be judged in relation to what is known or believed concerning its treatment of employees under a wide range of headings, its record in matters of health and safety, the impact of its operations on the environment, and on local communities and indigenous peoples, its demonstrated concern for human rights, and its dealings with partners, suppliers and overseas governments whose behaviour may itself be held in question. In all these respects, companies are now under permanent and often hostile scrutiny, and what are seen as failures or acts of misconduct on their part can be given immediate worldwide exposure.

This trend of events has presented a challenge to corporate

managements. Businesses everywhere have naturally responded; and in many cases, including particularly the more exposed MNEs, this has involved a thoroughgoing re-examination and re-orientation of objectives, policies, procedures and operating practices. Among these varied responses, it is possible to distinguish broadly two different schools of thought, two kinds of strategic thinking. Although representatives of both are apt to refer to 'corporate social responsibility', it is only in the second case that the doctrine is given its full meaning and takes the form of CSR.

The first school of thought comprises those firms, and organisations representing business, whose reaction might be described as *defensive and business focused*. It is defensive, in the sense that the changes that go with it are viewed, not so much as desirable for their own sake, but rather as necessary or prudent adaptations to a new and more demanding situation. It is business focused, in that in each case the rationale for the changes is derived entirely, or very largely, from a concern with the interests of the enterprise itself: it is not explicitly linked to some wider goal. Corporations are seen as needing to adapt because it makes good business sense for them to do so, and not because this would make the world a better place.

By contrast, the second type of reaction is *positive and broadly focused*. It is positive, in that the change in philosophy and practice, the new orientation of business, is seen in terms of recognising and grasping new opportunities, rather than – or as well as – adapting to outside forces. It is broadly focused, in that it identifies a new and enlarged responsibility for businesses today in contributing to both the wellbeing of society in general and the integrity of the natural environment. To emphasise 'social' responsibility in this way is not to neglect or disregard the interests of the business, but to place them in a wider context, to reassess them. Corporations are seen as having a leading role, in society and on the world stage, as agents of progress. This role (it is argued) needs to be recognised, made explicit, and given expression in the objectives that firms set themselves and in their policies and operations: businesses should embrace, and give effect to, the notion of *corporate citizenship*. It is from this way of thinking, this point of departure, that the full-fledged doctrine of CSR has taken shape.

Both individual firms and organisations representing businesses have increasingly adopted the second approach. Among the organisations, a leading instance is the World Business Council for Sustainable Development (WBCSD). The Council has become a highly influential body, and support for it is a good indication of the extent to which international corporations around the world have committed themselves to CSR. The membership has now risen to over 150 large MNEs drawn from 30 countries. They include ABB, AT&T, BHP, BP Amoco, Deloitte Touche Tomatsu, Ford, General Motors, Glaxo Wellcome, Mitsubishi, Monsanto, Nestlé, Procter and Gamble, Rio Tinto, Shell International, Sony, Time Warner, Toyota, Unilever and Volkswagen. Besides the main body, the WBCSD itself, there are also some national counterparts and a number of affiliated business organisations. Moreover, the WBCSD network is far from standing alone. Across the world, there are many other organisations, either made up of business firms or involving them, with similar objectives and beliefs and often overlapping membership. A prominent example, based in Britain but with an international list of participating firms, is the Prince of Wales Business Leaders Forum (hereafter PBLF). Its 60 or so corporate members include DIAGEO, Coca-Cola, ABB, Glaxo SmithKline, Mitsubishi,

Andersen Consulting, and Shell Transport and Trading. A parallel organisation, covering member countries of the European Union, is the European Business Network for Social Cohesion (hereafter EBNSC, though it has recently renamed itself CSR Europe), which comprises over 30 leading companies. In the United States, Business for Social Responsibility can be seen as a counterpart.

Outside the business world, the notion of CSR has gained attention, and often finds support, in a variety of places: among academics, including faculty members in business schools where increasingly the subject finds a place in the syllabus; in research centres and institutes, a growing number of which have been specifically established with a view to furthering the cause; from foundations; among journalists and commentators, including those writing in journals that are devoted to the subject; from the increasing number of investors and investment funds which are concerned to promote 'socially responsible investment' in companies; from within those NGOs that are not unrelentingly hostile to big business as such; in numerous political and governmental circles; and within a good many international agencies. Everywhere it appears to be gaining ground.

In Britain, a striking recent development has been the assignment to a minister in the present (Labour) government of formal responsibility for the oversight of corporate social responsibility across the country. In a speech on 4 May 2000, when his appointment was officially announced, the minister concerned, Dr Kim Howells, said that this new post embraced two key roles:

- Making the business case for CSR
- Co-ordinating government activity across Whitehall to promote CSR.

More recently, the government has set up a website 'to provide a forum where businesses can promote corporate social responsibility in a more effective manner'.

Despite these favourable references and the use of the initials, Her Majesty's Government has not by its actions endorsed the doctrine of CSR as defined here. In the new initiative just described, its main concern is with the role of business in local communities in Britain, with a strong emphasis on small and medium-sized firms: other dimensions of the idea are not explicitly brought in. All the same, it is significant that a British government has been ready to give its blessing to both the general notion and the label. Moreover, this recent move fits with other steps which the government has taken in the same direction. These include the Ethical Trading Initiative (to encourage British firms to ensure the observance by their overseas suppliers of 'core labour standards'), the creation in the Foreign and Commonwealth Office of a Global Citizenship Unit (to enlist business support in the conduct of British foreign policy), and the establishment by the Department for International Development of a Business Partnership Unit (to promote business co-operation in meeting goals for reducing poverty in developing countries). Although the government's official line is that 'corporate responsibility and citizenship should be a business-driven agenda', it is clear that it wishes to further the trend towards these.

In the European Union as a whole, evidence of the same disposition is to be seen in the official support given by member governments, at the European summit meeting held in Lisbon in March 2000, to a proposal for what has been described as 'a major campaign aimed at persuading companies to take ... CSR issues more seriously'. The proposal came from the EBNSC, together with the

Copenhagen Centre which shares the same goals: the two organisations submitted a 'Business Leaders' Input' to the summit, entitled *For an Entrepreneurial and Inclusive Europe* (hereafter referred to as the BLI Report). In this case what is in question is CSR as here defined. As to the next stages within the EU, it has been announced that the government of Belgium, which took over the presidency in June 2001, is to take CSR as one of its leading themes for consideration by member governments and other agencies: a major conference on CSR and socially responsible investment is to be convened in November 2001. Alongside and reinforcing these initiatives, the European Commission's Directorate-General of Employment and Social Affairs has recently issued a consultative document, a Green Paper, on how to promote the adoption of CSR by ministries across the EU. (I comment on this document in Part 8 below.)

A notable official endorsement of the general principle has recently come from the member governments – now 30 in number – of the Organisation for Economic Cooperation and Development (OECD). At the OECD Ministerial Council meeting of 2000, ministers approved a revised version of the Organisation's *Guidelines for Multinational Enterprises*. The guidelines are 'recommendations on responsible business conduct addressed by governments to [MNEs]'; and as such, 'They represent standards of behaviour supplemental to applicable law', and are designed 'to prove a useful reference point and tool *for promoting corporate social responsibility*' (italics mine).[1] Admittedly, this is a broad statement only:

---

1   The quotations are from the Statement by the Chairman of the Ministerial Council meeting, who was the Australian Treasurer, Peter Costello. The statement provides an introduction (pp. 5–6) to the new *Guidelines*. These have also been endorsed by the governments of three countries that are not OECD members – Argentina, Brazil and Chile.

the wording here does not necessarily imply endorsement of CSR. Even so, the use of the phrase is significant, and still more so is the explicit reiteration by OECD governments that MNEs should think of themselves as subject to obligations which go beyond, though remaining consistent with, the laws that apply to them in the countries where they operate.

The many official high-level statements favouring the general principle of corporate social responsibility not only lend it authority, but also reinforce the incentives for businesses and business organisations to be seen to have adopted it. For one thing, this may help to improve their standing with governments. Again, they may calculate that taking action themselves, along lines that are broadly approved by governments, will reduce the likelihood of having irksome regulations imposed on them. Under both headings, their moves have to be presented as a positive and creative departure, rather than a grudging exercise in damage limitation. The emphasis has to be on the virtues and benefits of corporate citizenship, and on the readiness of enterprises to embrace it of their own accord.

Among its sources of allegiance, the subject of corporate social responsibility generally, and today's CSR in particular, has now given rise to its own specialised cadres of expertise. Here three main overlapping areas are involved. One is the academic world, with the growth of course work and research in CSR-related topics. In this connection European business leaders, in the BLI Report (p. 10), recommend

> The development of a European initiative to encourage
> universities and business schools to create, expand and
> diversify graduate, executive and post-graduate courses in
> CSR, corporate citizenship and business ethics.

A recent development along these lines has been the establishment in Britain, at the University of Nottingham, of an International Centre for Corporate Social Responsibility.

A second newly arisen and expanding area of pro-CSR professional involvement is that of institutions to promote 'ethical and social investment'. A recent issue of the British newsletter *Ethical Performance* lists under the heading of 'ethical and ecological' 53 UK unit trusts, 29 UK insurance funds, and 57 investment funds in continental Europe. Bringing in North America would greatly extend this list. The purpose of such funds is to identify firms, products and lines of activity which either meet or fail to meet tests of ethical, social and environmental acceptability, and from this to advise investors and offer opportunities for them. Like many of the NGOs, whose views and aspirations are often close to theirs, such funds may bring pressure to bear on companies to endorse CSR and act in accordance with it. In Britain, official encouragement for this trend was provided in the Welfare Reform and Pensions Act of 1999, which made it obligatory for pension funds to disclose whether they are taking into account social, environmental and ethical considerations in their choice of investments. In France, a forthcoming law will require fund managers of employee savings plans to state their position with respect to 'socially responsible' investment.

Alongside these elements, and mingling with them, substantial and increasing numbers of a new breed of consultants and expert advisers now stand ready, whether as employees or outsiders, to assist businesses in the task of defining and giving effect to CSR in their operations, and in monitoring and evaluating their progress. In this context, the suggestion has even been made that a new profession is in course of being born.

As against this general trend towards acceptance, advocacy and diffusion of CSR, dissenting or even sceptical voices appear to be very much in the minority. It is true that, even in the ranks of MNEs, not all have signed the pledge; and among the firms that have responded to the new pressures and challenges there must be many, perhaps even a majority, whose reactions fall more into the first category referred to above, as defensive and business focused. But there is little sign of overt opposition to CSR from within the business community. Outside it, there have been many attacks on stakeholder theory, to which it is related, but CSR as such seems up to now to have provoked fewer enemies. (A noteworthy exception is Robert Halfon, in his incisive Social Affairs Unit paper entitled *Corporate Irresponsibility: Is business appeasing anti-business activists?*) One reason for taking CSR seriously is that it seems now to have achieved something close to a consensus. This itself is novel. In the past history of debates concerning the role and social responsibilities of business, no other approach, no other way of thinking, has won such broad support, whether among businesses or more generally.

3 DEFINING AND INTERPRETING CSR

Although much has been written about corporate social responsibility, there is to my knowledge no standard agreed presentation, no authoritative textbook treatment, of CSR as here defined. However, useful up-to-date guidance from within the business world itself is to be found in various publications by firms and business organisations, including statements of corporate policy and speeches by chief executive officers (CEOs) and other leading business figures. Two sources in particular are helpful, though as will be seen there is much to query in both.

First, the WBCSD has published the report of a special and far-reaching inquiry that it launched in 1998 with a view 'to providing a better understanding of what corporate social responsibility means and what represents good practice'. This task was undertaken by a working group in which no less than 85 member companies participated. After issuing an interim report in 1999, the group engaged in a series of 'global stakeholder dialogues', following which they brought out their final report this year. It is entitled *Corporate Social Responsibility: making good business sense*. I refer to it here as WBC2000, and to its predecessor, the interim report, as WBC1999.

Second, one of the international businesses which has moved farthest in rethinking its aims and operations is the Royal Dutch/Shell Group (hereafter 'Shell'). The present Chairman of the Committee of Managing Directors of the group, Sir Mark Moody-Stuart, begins his preface to a recent company leaflet by saying:

> Shell is undergoing fundamental change. We are creating a transformation in every part of the Group to make us more efficient and flexible for our customers and the marketplace. But beyond that we have appraised both our role as a major multinational group and the expectations that society places on us. (Shell International, *Listening and Responding*)

As part of this process of transformation, Shell has set out its new company philosophy and codes of practice in a number of publications. Of these, the most comprehensive are four successive annual 'Shell Reports', entitled respectively *Profits and Principles: does there have to be a choice?* (referred to here as SR98), *People, Planet and Profits: an act of commitment* (SR99), *How Do We Stand? People, planet and profits* (SR2000), and *People, planet and profits: The Shell Report* (SR2001). Although these reports and other company statements do not emphasise CSR as such, they in fact give expression to its ideas; and indeed, a senior Shell executive, Philip Watts, who has been designated as the next Chairman of the Committee of Managing Directors, was co-chairman of the WBCSD working group just referred to, which produced the two reports on CSR.

WBC2000 notes on the opening page of its main text (p. 4) that 'a universally accepted definition of CSR has yet to emerge'. However, it offers considered guidance on the three main related aspects of the doctrine: its underlying purpose or rationale; the nature of the commitment that it involves; and the broad implications for what businesses should actually do to give expression to it.

Under the first heading, the emphasis is on the contribution that corporations make, or can make, to a better future: '... business is part of the solution to creating a more stable, healthy and prosperous world' (p. 2). From this role, this primary mission, the report goes on (p. 3) to define 'The fundamentals of ... CSR' as 'maximising the long-term contribution of business to society and taking care to minimise adverse impacts'. It will be seen that at this level of generality the notions of profitability and return to shareholders do not enter in.

The goal of sustainable development

Against this background, the report sets out (p. 10) the revised agreed summary definition of CSR that emerged from the working group's long process of inquiry, discussion and consultation:

> Corporate social responsibility is the commitment of
> business to contribute to sustainable development, working
> with employees, their families, the local community and
> society at large to improve their quality of life.

Here pride of place is given to the notion of sustainable development. It forms the basis, the point of departure, for the way in which CSR is viewed and defined by most if not all of the many firms, business organisations and outside commentators that have endorsed it. In the words of WBC99 (p. 3), 'CSR is an integral part of sustainable development'.

A growing number of corporations have made explicit commitments along these lines. For example

- Shell has said that 'We will embrace the concept of

sustainable development in our business decisions, large and small' (SR99, inside front cover).

- The President and CEO of Dow Chemical, William Stavropoulos, in a speech delivered in October 2000, referred to 'making sustainability a way of life, a constant journey without an end point', and later to 'embedding sustainability goals and principles into the core strategies of each of our companies'.

- The Chairman and CEO of DuPont, Chad Holliday, in a speech delivered in May 2000, said of his firm that 'As we think about the new century, we have determined that our central focus must be on "sustainable growth" ... [which] is our operational definition of sustainable development'.

This consensus across the member companies accounts for the emphasis on sustainable development in the two WBCSD reports. The CSR message is that companies can best carry out their mission to improve the world by endorsing the aim of sustainable development and directing their efforts and activities to furthering it.

Despite the considerable weight thus placed on it, the notion of sustainable development is not defined or spelled out in the two WBCSD reports, nor in other business publications that make use of it. In these documents as elsewhere, reference is often made to the summary formula that was offered in the 1987 report of the United Nations World Commission on Environment and Development (the 'Brundtland Report'), which recommended that sustainable development 'should be seen as a global objective'. The Report asserted (p. 40) that 'Sustainable development seeks to meet the needs and aspirations of the present without compromising the ability to meet those of the future'. This form of words, however, though endlessly quoted across the world, is no more than a statement of general principle which in itself offers no guide to action.[1]

One way of taking further the idea of sustainable development, which has now been widely adopted not just in the business world but also more generally, is to define it with reference to what are said to be its three aspects or dimensions. These have been identified as *economic, environmental* and *social*.[2] In the words of WBC2000 (p. 2), sustainable development 'requires the integration of social, environmental and economic considerations to make balanced judgements for the long term'. Similarly, SR98 refers (p. 36) to 'the idea of sustainable development, which gives equal weight to economic progress, environmental protection and social responsibility'. This formulation is often seen as providing a basis, a framework, for spelling out the practical implications of a business commitment to CSR. Firms are enjoined to organise and direct their activities towards promoting sustainable development under all three headings, and to establish for this purpose an explicit accounting and reporting process, so that the net contribution to all three goals can be identified and at least roughly assessed. To quote again the WBC2000 report (p. 16), 'Companies . . . need to demonstrate, more quickly and with increasing levels

---

1   The Brundtland Report has more to say on the subject, but it is the formula quoted here which has caught on.

2   A word of elucidation is needed here. In the world of CSR, as indeed more generally, 'social' is used in both an all-embracing and a specific sense. In the term 'corporate social responsibility' it refers to all three dimensions that sustainable development is thought to embrace. But it is also applied more narrowly to one of these dimensions – that is the 'social' as distinct from the 'economic' and the 'environmental'.

of detail, that their operations enhance economic development, ensure environmental protection and promote social equity.'

Such an approach raises questions which the twin WBCSD reports, and other documents of the same kind, do not answer or even consider directly. *How is it possible for a firm to 'demonstrate', or even to be sure itself, that its policies and operations promote the goals of 'economic development, environmental protection, and social equity'?* What are the criteria for judging this, and on whose authority are they decided? How are these goals to be defined and given content? How far should corporations develop in this context their own definitions, rules and standards, or should they be looking to governments or public opinion for guidance, or to legislation for instructions? Only if the three goals were all well defined, and if every one broadly agreed on how they could best be realised by businesses and others, would these questions have ready and uncontroversial answers.

In effect, though not in so many words, this is what exponents of CSR presume: they speak and write as though both ends and means were broadly agreed. In particular, they take it for granted that the notion of sustainable development is well defined and unexceptionable, so that, both as a principle and as a guide to action, it embodies a worldwide consensus of right-thinking persons. As to the idea itself, Sir Mark Moody-Stuart, in his introduction to the Shell leaflet already quoted, writes that 'the principles of sustainable development are irrefutable'. As to practical implications, there is little to suggest, in the business and business-related publications cited here, that there might be problems or differences of view in identifying the kinds of actions that have to be taken, under all three headings, in order to ensure that what firms do will promote sustainable development. Hence the answer implicitly given to the challenge from authors such as Milton Friedman, when they argue that managers have no right to determine for themselves what is in the 'social interest', is that no such right is in fact claimed. In embracing CSR, corporations can be viewed as aligning themselves with beliefs, values and objectives which are generally accepted, by governments and public opinion alike. There is neither conflict nor usurpation of roles.

A hollow consensus

This presumption of agreement is understandable, in so far as the general notion of sustainable development has today many friends across the world, and relatively few enemies or critics. It is now widely proclaimed, in both official and unofficial circles, as a leading or dominant objective, while the threefold division into economic, environmental and social aspects has likewise become part of general usage. As to governments, a notable illustration is to be found in the communiqué issued at the end of the 1999 meeting of the OECD Ministerial Council. This included the statement that:

> The pursuit of sustainable development . . . is a key
> objective for OECD countries. Achieving this objective
> requires the integration of economic, environmental and
> social considerations into policy-making, in particular by
> the internalisation of costs, and the development and
> diffusion of environmentally sound technologies worldwide.

What is more, OECD governments have explicitly called on international businesses to think in these same terms. In the newly revised *OECD Guidelines for Multinational Enterprises*, referred to above, item 1 under the heading of 'General Policies' (p. 19) specifies that enterprises should 'Contribute to economic, social and environmental progress with a view to achieving sustainable development'.

Given the widespread allegiance to the concept of sustainable development thus interpreted, and the extent of outside support for the view that it should be explicitly endorsed by enterprises, it would be surprising if the business world had held itself apart. As it is, the companies that have embraced the principle, and taken it as the basis for redefining their role and their conception of their social responsibilities, can think of themselves as having fallen into line with a near-universal consensus. They can be portrayed as playing their assigned part in a worldwide team effort, involving governments, international agencies, businesses and NGOs, to promote a shared objective which no reasonable person could now call in question.

Despite appearances, however, such a presumption of agreement is not warranted. Although sustainable development – like corporate social responsibility itself – is an appealing formula, which has indeed been widely endorsed, there are differences of opinion as to what it ought to mean and what it should be taken to imply in practice, while the whole notion is questioned or rejected by some. There is no solid and well-developed consensus which provides a basis for action, whether by governments or by businesses.

One source of disagreement relates to the very notion of what is to be sustained. On the one hand, there are those who think of this in relation to human beings: their sole or main concern is with the sustainable welfare of people, now and for the future. By contrast, others think in terms of ecosystems rather than humanity, so that sustainability is identified with ecosystem resilience. In the 2000 BBC Reith Lectures in Britain, for which

'Sustainable Development' was the title, the leader of the Southern California Sierra Club, during the discussion that followed one of the lectures, argued that sustainable development 'has become a buzz-word for human centred destruction of the wild planet'. Such a view is common among environmentalists and their NGOs.

In so far as human welfare is taken to be the criterion, the accepted notion that there are three distinct aspects of sustainable development, for which in any case a rationale is hard to find, itself becomes open to question.[3] Here again, the appearance of agreement is deceptive.

On one approach at any rate, these are not three separate watertight categories: to a large extent, though no doubt not entirely, both 'social' and 'environmental' aspects can be subsumed under 'economic'. As to the former, the distribution of income and wealth, and more broadly of material welfare, is clearly an economic phenomenon (just as the composition of output is), and policies designed to influence it are economic policies. Hence in so far as 'social' aspects relate to this distribution, which is often the case, they do not fall into a category of their own. (Even on this, however, there are dissenting views.) As to the latter, different states of the environment can be thought of as being compared and evaluated with reference to the value placed on them by economic agents, as judged by estimated willingness to pay at the margin. In this way of thinking, the state of the environment enters into the conception, and as far as possible the measurement,

---

3 In a recent book by a group of economists entitled *Measuring Sustainable Development* (Atkinson *et al.*, 1997), the laconic statement is made on the second page that 'The concept of sustainable development now includes economic, social and environmental requirements (Munasinghe 1993)'. But on consulting the work thus recommended, I could find no convincing grounds for the threefold division.

of the economic (or material) welfare of people. Such an approach, however, is often strongly contested by environmentalists: this too is an area of dispute.

If and in so far as the economic aspect is taken to be dominant, it is debatable whether the notion of sustainable development adds much if anything to the long-accepted formula that a leading objective of public policy is to promote and increase material welfare, with due regard to how it is distributed both between rich and poor and between those now living and those to come. The emperor's new clothes appear as the old outfit with some unnecessary or questionable trimmings. Among the latter is the idea that sustainability as such is necessarily to be pursued or insisted on.[4]

Such basic issues, and the disagreements surrounding them, are not referred to in CSR-related writings, which take the goal of sustainable development, and its three supposed dimensions, as given and established. Further, where such documents spell out what sustainable development actually involves, agreement is likewise presumed in relation to policies or courses of action which in fact may be open to different interpretations or to objection. On the 'economic' side, for example, a stated goal for some firms is support for local contractors and suppliers, so that the case for protection is simply assumed to be valid despite the arguments that can be brought against it. In relation to the 'environmental' aspect, many MNEs have announced commitments such as pursuing 'eco-efficiency', minimising wastes, discharges, emissions, effluents and spills, and promoting biodiversity. Under the heading of 'social', they have pledged themselves to protect and enlarge

---

4   An argument on these lines is presented by Wilfred Beckerman in Chapter 9 of his book *Small Is Stupid*, published in the United States under the title *Through Green-Colored Glasses*.

human rights, to raise standards of occupational health and safety, and to promote 'diversity' in the context of human resources policies. All these allegedly 'non-economic' undertakings, thus stated, have the air of virtue; but in every case there are issues of definition, of degree, and of weighing costs and benefits at the margin, and these are typically glossed over in standard presentations both by companies and in business-related publications. As further noted below, it is possible that actions under all these headings will do more harm than good.

When it comes to 'environmental' and (still more) 'social' goals, CSR-related statements sometimes take the form simply of listing objectives or courses of action which the companies or the authors concerned have decided (albeit not in isolation) to endorse, even though these are far from being agreed by everyone. Thus, for example

- Shell have taken the position (in SR2000, p. 12) that 'Sustainable development offers a means of tackling some of society's most pressing concerns – extremes of poverty and wealth, population growth, human rights, environmental destruction, climate change and loss of biodiversity.'
- In the 1997 report of a High-Level Advisory Group to the Secretary-General of the OECD it is laid down (p. 8) that 'sustainable development reaches into the issues of minority rights, women's rights, and, given the focus on the needs of future generations, children's rights'. (Within this group, a co-chairman was Stephan Schmidheiny, founder of the Business Council for Sustainable Development – the title 'World' was added later – while one of the members was the Secretary-General of the

International Chamber of Commerce, Maria Livanos-Cattaui.)

- Tom Gladwin, professor at the Graduate School of Business at the University of Michigan, has taken the view that 'Socio-economic sustainability' involves 'poverty alleviation, population stabilisation, female empowerment, human rights observance and opportunity on a massive scale' (quoted in Mitchell, 1998: 52).

Whatever the case for listing these various goals, they are not all self-evidently well defined and valid, and some are clearly contentious. In a number of cases, if not all, their connection with sustainability is unclear. They are far from embodying a worldwide consensus.

Whether made subject to such dubious interpretations or left ill defined, the present notion of sustainable development is an inadequate basis for rewriting business ethics, reforming corporate governance, and redefining the scope and purpose of corporations today. Contrary to what is widely claimed or assumed, its adoption by businesses, business organisations and business commentators does not in itself mark an advance in corporate thinking. The case for endorsing CSR is neither established nor clarified by stating it in these terms.

The 'triple bottom line'

A commitment by businesses to sustainable development, under what are taken to be its three distinct aspects, goes in some cases, probably an increasing number, with endorsing the notion of the so-called *triple bottom line*. This implies extending the traditional accounting 'bottom line', which shows overall net profitability as a money figure, so as to encompass all the three aspects. Although the general notion of a triple bottom line seems to have taken hold and to be gaining ground, there are probably wide differences in the way in which it is interpreted; nor would this be surprising, since the approach is still new and experimental and different firms face different circumstances and problems. Here again, a broad distinction may be useful: the idea of meeting the triple bottom line can be interpreted either loosely and metaphorically, or more strictly.

On a loose interpretation, a firm explicitly recognises an obligation to meet specified goals that have been identified as 'economic', 'environmental' or 'social'; it translates this where possible into actual commitments or targets to be met; and it institutes reporting procedures with a view to monitoring results and learning from experience. Increasingly, MNEs have moved down this path, and introduced new or more elaborate management systems in consequence. Since financial reporting is well developed, it is under the other two headings that new departures have chiefly been made. Among many examples that might be quoted, BP Amoco now issues an annual Environmental and Social Report, and BHP an annual Environment and Community Report. In recent issues, both these documents have reported on (1) occupational health and safety within the firm, (2) commitments made, and results achieved, in relation to environmental goals or targets, such as reducing emissions, and (3) relations with local communities where the firms are operating, and actions undertaken and expenditures made for the benefit of these communities. The BP Amoco report, being more explicitly 'social', also covers general policies towards employees and concern for human rights. In both cases facts, figures and results are cited, and the BHP report in particular carries appendices which go into some detail. In neither case, however, is there any pretence that a social or environmental 'bottom line' can be expressed numerically, and indeed the distinction between the two categories is not made at all rigorously. This way of proceeding may well be typical.

By contrast, some large companies have made a commitment to go much farther towards translating the idea of the triple bottom line into a set of explicit corporate objectives embodied in new and expanded systems of accounting and reporting. Here again, two instances are Dow Chemical and Shell. In the former case, Mr Stavropoulos, in the speech already quoted, reported that

> As we pursue Business Excellence, we are measuring our
> success against a number of metrics, which address key
> aspects of the triple bottom-line, and tying our
> compensation programs to the achievements of these
> metrics . . .

As for Shell, the company has stated (in SR98, p. 50) that

> We shall . . . seek to develop an approach to calculating the
> 'net value' which Group companies add to the world in a
> given time frame by taking into account our contribution to
> the three components of sustainable development.

Action on these lines has in fact been taken. On a later page of SR98, in an invited contribution, John Elkington, chairman of a consulting firm called SustainAbility, notes that

> Shell International has now assembled an internal Social
> Accountability Team, pooling resources with Arthur D.
> Little and SustainAbility, to develop a range of 'net value
> added' metrics. The indicators will be developed with inputs
> from Shell's internal and external stakeholders. (pp. 46–7)

From this it would appear that *Shell have seriously embarked on a company-wide project the aim of which is to measure, with a view to maximising, the firm's net contribution to the welfare of the world.* How far other companies may join it in a similarly bold undertaking is unclear; but the possibilities for doing so are now the subject of widespread debate and research, and increasingly of experiment, within the business community and business-focused institutions. Among other things, this has opened up a promising new area of business for management consultants.

Giving effect to CSR

Whether or not a conscious attempt is made to put into operation the triple bottom line, CSR involves the adoption and development not only of explicit new commitments but also of new procedures. An integral feature of the proposed CSR regime is that it prescribes closer and more systematic contact with a range of outside groups and interests which have been identified as stakeholders. To quote again from WBC2000, 'The essence of corporate social responsibility is to recognise the value of external stakeholder dialogue ... We place stakeholder engagement at the center of CSR activity' (p. 15). The report then offers an illustrative list of stakeholders. This extends (1) within the firm, to both shareholders and employees, and (2) outside it, to business partners, suppliers, competitors, government regulators, NGOs and pressure groups, and local communities. Nor is this all: earlier in the document (p. 3), both 'government at various levels' and 'intergovernmental organizations' are likewise mentioned in the same connection. From this standpoint, shareholders appear as just one of many groups whose views have to be taken into account, and with whom there should be continuing 'dialogue'.

At the end of the WBC2000 report (pp. 24-5), a two-page 'self-assessment questionnaire' is provided to enable firms 'to gauge how well your company is engaging CSR'. For full compliance, a business should have:

- A written 'vision', prepared in consultation with stakeholders.
- A formal commitment to CSR, with a board member made responsible for CSR policy.
- A statement of corporate values, formulated in consultation with stakeholders, approved by the board, and communicated to employees.
- A code of conduct 'for ensuring adherence to corporate values'.
- A full listing of its stakeholders, a clear understanding of its relationship to them, and a list of issues, agreed with them, in which they and the company are jointly involved.
- A procedure by which it 'has assessed the social and ethical impacts' of its products or services and its operations.
- A 'CSR policy' governing implementation, agreed with stakeholders and communicated to employees.
- 'A program for monitoring CSR policy', with targets and timescales for improvement.
- Procedures for measuring and monitoring performance against targets.
- Systems for reporting progress to employees, the public, and 'other stakeholder groups'. (Such reports should 'fully address all the issues identified in dialogue with stakeholders'.)
- A process for independent review of such company reporting.

- A process by which it 'continuously reviews and updates CSR strategy', in conjunction with stakeholders.
- Support systems for 'measurement and auditing of CSR performance'. These should include a system for 'collecting stakeholder input' and 'an internal audit program'.

In the light of such a list, it is not surprising to read the judgement made by Shell, in SR98 (p. 47), that the adoption of CSR 'demands a deep shift in corporate culture, values, decision-making processes and behaviour'.

New horizons

These proposed changes, in objectives and procedures alike, raise basic issues in business ethics, corporate governance, and the economics of public policy. Interpreted in the ways outlined above, CSR appears as a radical and possibly historic new departure. It is true that not all is new. Past business history provides many instances in which firms have chosen to support particular causes or programmes outside their main operations, even though, on the surface at least, such actions could be seen as reducing the return to shareholders. Again, and as noted already, the general notion of corporate social responsibility goes a long way back, and the idea that a firm's success may depend in part on its reputation for open-handedness and fair dealing, for good treatment of its employees, and for taking explicit account of the public interest, is far from novel. But today's CSR, as sketched out above, appears as more systematic and far reaching than earlier thinking and practice. It establishes the wellbeing of 'society', rather than profitability and the interests of its owners, as the primary concern of a business; it incorporates ideas that are partly novel on how this objective is to be viewed and interpreted; it points towards specific organisational goals, and with them measures of performance, which are not defined with reference to profitability; and it links the pursuit of these wider goals to more elaborate operating procedures and forms of corporate governance in which, among other consequences, the status of owners would be effectively downgraded. What is more, it offers a pattern, a model, for all businesses to follow. All this goes well beyond the numerous and varied individual packages of conspicuous good works, special employee benefits, targeted sponsorship exercises and active public relations policies which have long been part of the corporate scene. Taking CSR seriously could well bring substantial changes to the companies involved; and the possibility that the business world in general might go down this path, as the many advocates of CSR propose, raises new and far-reaching concerns.

4 CAPITALISM MADE ANEW: THE CSR BLUEPRINT

At the level of the individual firm, a leading question is how the adoption of CSR might affect the profitability of a business and its obligations to those who own it, the shareholders. Sir Samuel Brittan has made the point that:

> There is a systematic ambiguity . . . in nearly all the talk
> about socially responsible business. Do these proponents
> claim that these extra activities will indeed help a business's
> long-term profitability? Or do they assert that a business
> should follow other objectives? (Brittan, 1995: 40)

How does the doctrine of CSR measure up to this challenge?

CSR and profitability: grounds for concern

Before looking at some responses that have been given, the point has to be made that embracing CSR would inevitably have consequences that would raise the costs of doing business, could well reduce revenues, and might also cause companies to sponsor low-yielding investments which they would otherwise have turned down. To that extent it would reduce profits, *both in the short term and over a longer period*; and except in cases where shareholders knew of this, and were approving or acquiescent, it would be contrary to their interests. As against this, however, a public and whole-hearted commitment to CSR could also have positive effects on sales and revenues, and indeed on some aspects of costs as well; and these might tilt the balance so that the net impact on profitability was favourable. Both sides of the account have to be considered.

On the negative side, one has only to look at the list of innovations in company practice that CSR involves, as set out above from WBC2000, to see that cost increases, possibly substantial, would result from these alone. The main factors here are (1) the wider range of goals and concerns that would bear on management at all levels, (2) the need to devise and maintain more elaborate accounting and reporting systems, with new cadres of expertise, and (3) the involvement of management in new time-consuming consultation, negotiation and review processes with a range of outside groups, many of them unconcerned with the commercial success of the business in question and some of them deeply hostile or suspicious. These factors would operate in all firms that adopted CSR whole heartedly; and indeed, the additional demands on management would probably have unfavourable effects on the revenue side as well.

That such possibilities are more than speculative can be seen from a recent specific example. One of the international companies that most conspicuously and enthusiastically embraced the ideas of CSR was Levi Strauss. Indeed, it has sometimes been held up as a shining example for others to follow. An instance of this is to be found in Michael Hopkins's book *The Planetary Bargain*, where the author (who is Professor of Corporate and Social Research at Middlesex University) looks forward to 'a new world' of 'socially responsible enterprises'. He suggests (p. 195) that:

As this new world takes shape, large enterprises will be

> more socially responsible than many governments ... The
> startling social responsiveness of Levi Strauss to its suppliers
> and employees, for example, exceeds that of many nation
> states ... Companies like Levi Strauss and Body Shop will
> be the rule, not the exception as now.

As luck would have it, Hopkins's book must have gone to press just too late for him to take account of an article by Nina Munk which appeared in *Fortune* magazine in April 1999. The article is headed 'How Levi's Trashed a Great American Brand', and it tells a sad story of declining sales, profits and share value. Levi Strauss is described (p. 34) as 'a failed utopian management experiment'; and the failure is directly attributed to the fact that the then CEO, Robert Haas, 'was intent on showing that a company driven by social values could outperform a company hostage to profits alone' (p. 33). This episode suggests that it is not only through pushing up costs, but also by eroding the commercial effectiveness of management, that subscribing overzealously to CSR can make a company less competent in carrying out its primary task of serving the wishes, tastes and interests of its customers.[1]

Of course, this is one instance only, which should not necessarily be viewed as representative. Advocates of CSR would no doubt take the position that its adoption need not, and is certainly not intended to, distract managers from their primary commercial roles or weaken their overall performance. All the same, the possibility that new, more elaborate and less focused ways of conduct-

---

1   The present CEO of Levi Strauss was recently able to announce that the new management had 'gained control of the business' and was 'on track to stem its declining sales in the coming year'. The dollar value of sales was reported to have fallen by almost 25 per cent between 1998 and 2000 (*Financial Times*, 11 January, 2001).

ing business will raise costs and diminish revenues cannot just be set aside.

In addition to these factors, costs are almost certain to be pushed up – though much may depend on circumstances – in so far as businesses, in the pursuit of CSR, go beyond their legal obligations under the following headings:

- Adopting policies and practices designed to limit the environmental impact of their operations, as for example in the targets which firms such as Dow, Shell and BP Amoco have set themselves for emissions reductions.
- Adopting norms and standards relating to (1) the environment and (2) occupational health and safety, especially where within MNEs these are applied uniformly across national borders.
- Adopting uniform company-wide norms and standards relating to employment and working conditions, even when local circumstances are widely different.
- More generally, offering wages, salaries and terms and conditions of employment which are not closely related to local market conditions.
- Systematically fixing and achieving norms and targets for 'diversity' in relation to recruitment, selection and promotion within the firm (both Dow and Shell have embraced the principle of diversity).
- Giving preferences, formal or informal, to local suppliers and contractors.
- Giving preferences to particular suppliers as a way of promoting 'equal opportunity', as in the case of Shell Oil of the United States, which 'has a target to spend 10 per cent of

its expenditure [excluding raw materials] with supplying companies owned by women or people from ethnic minorities' (SR2000, p. 13).

- Refusing to buy from firms whose business practices are viewed as unacceptable, as for example in the case of Shell, whose companies 'do not work with suppliers and contractors who are not able to meet Shell standards' (SR98, p. 13).

- Refusing to enter into joint ventures where prospective partners have what are viewed as unacceptably low standards: here again, 'Shell companies will no longer form joint ventures where partners decline to adopt Business Principles compatible with ours' (SR98, p. 38).

Just as meeting such self-chosen environmental or 'social' targets would probably raise costs to businesses, so it might lead them to make investments or product choices which in the end prove low yielding, in so far as their primary rationale is not that of profitability. DuPont is an example. In the address already quoted, Chad Holliday noted that, with a view to reducing its 'environmental footprint', the firm has

... set two major goals for the year 2010 ... The first is a goal to source 10% of our total global energy needs from renewable energy. The second is to derive 25 per cent of our revenues from non-depletable sources.

Again, both Shell and BP Amoco have embarked on programmes (1) to reduce their flaring of natural gas, (2) to convert their refineries to produce cleaner fuels, and (3) to increase their involvement in the development and production of renewable energy sources.

Of course, it can be argued that any or all of the various actions listed above might prove to be commercially worthwhile, once their full effects, on costs and revenues together, were taken into account. They could also be defended as socially desirable, and hence incumbent on responsible businesses, even if their expected impact on profits was questionable or negative. But the fact remains that *in themselves* they tend, or may tend, to reduce profitability – by inflating costs, reducing revenues, and bringing returns on investment below threshold levels. Even if such effects are more than offset by favourable influences, their existence is not to be denied.

Typically, these aspects are glossed over in publications that argue the case for CSR, both within business and outside. Despite the frequent references in such documents to the need for greater openness and transparency, they show in this respect a pervasive lack of candour. Instead, the emphasis is almost entirely on the positive side.

CSR and profitability: the case in favour

A dominant theme of the advocates of CSR is that its adoption will be good for profits: there need be no conflict between a company's pursuing the objective of sustainable development, along the lines sketched out above, and serving the interests of its owners. Here are some characteristic expressions of this view from within the business world:

- 'CSR is increasingly being viewed, not only as making good business sense but also [as] contributing to the long-term prosperity of companies and ultimately its survival' (WBC2000, p. 3).

- 'CSR is essential to the long term prosperity of companies as it provides the opportunity to demonstrate the human face of business . . . ' (WBC2000, p. 6).
- '. . . sustainable development builds the platform on which business thrives and society prospers. Indeed, within the Royal Dutch/Shell group we have an absolute conviction that sustainable development is the fundamental driver for our own long-term business success' (Sir Mark Moody-Stuart of Shell, in his foreword to a *Financial Times* guide to 'Responsible Investment', 1999).
- 'When companies hitch their wagon to the star of sustainability, everyone is a winner' (William Stavropoulos of Dow Chemical, in the speech already quoted).
- '. . . corporate social responsibility is rooted in hard-headed business logic' (Greg Bourne, Regional Director, BP Amoco Australia and New Zealand, in a speech of February 1999).

Assertions of much the same kind are to be found in the writings of the many advocates of CSR – academics, commentators and others – outside the business world.

In arguing thus, both business persons and outsiders stress in particular the importance of two interrelated influences on the financial viability and wellbeing of a business, namely *expectations* and *reputation*. In WBC2000 it is argued (p. 7) that 'Understanding and taking account of society's expectations is quite simply enlightened self-interest for business in today's interdependent world'. Shell take the view that 'Sustainable development is a way of developing and safeguarding our reputation and it will help us develop our business in line with society's needs and expectations' (SR98, inside front cover). Among the outsider commentators quoted here, Christopher Marsden and Jörg Andriof, in a paper on 'corporate citizenship', argue that 'the sustainable pursuit of profits ... will increasingly depend on ecologically sound resource stewardship and a reputation for fair dealing with all "stakeholders"'. (Marsden was formerly Director of the Centre for Corporate Citizenship at the Warwick University Business School.)

In some companies, the views and expectations of employees are a leading consideration. This has clearly been a factor at Shell, and it has been especially emphasised in speeches by the CEO of BP Amoco, Sir John Browne.[2] In the 'keynote address' to a conference on corporate citizenship held in London in November 1999, Sir John referred to 'two key factors which are driving change at the moment'. One of these is outside expectations – 'what the world expects of companies – and especially, of large, international companies ... [People] expect them to behave as leading citizens in a complex world.' The 'second driver when it comes to corporate citizenship' is 'internal expectations': 'the views of the people within the company have a significant effect on what we do'. In particular, BP Amoco needs to recruit and keep talented executives who are looking for a job which besides personal advancement 'gives them the chance to contribute to the progress of society'.

Now in assessing where the balance will lie, when all the various influences on company profits are taken into account, the judgement of companies themselves has unquestionably to be given a lot of weight. If the members of the WBCSD and its affiliates and associates round the world, and a good many other businesses too, are

2   Sir John is now Lord Browne, having been raised to the peerage in April 2001. Here, however, I refer to him under the title that he held at the time he made the various contributions I have quoted, at this point and below.

convinced that CSR and profitability march together, it may appear presumptuous for an outsider to question them. The appearance of presumption becomes all the stronger when, as is indeed the case, an array of outside commentators could be called as witnesses on the side of these companies, while their shareholders appear to have accepted the various moves towards CSR with equanimity or even approval. However, this is not the end of the matter: there are grounds here for both scepticism and concern.

Construing expectations

One reason for doubt relates to the treatment of public opinion and expectations. Granted, it is true that if a good many people and organisations – including governments and official agencies, NGOs, trade unions, and businesses themselves in growing numbers, as well as numerous individuals – hold definite and similar views as to how companies should behave, if they are prepared to rate and judge particular companies in terms of conformity with the standards thus set or implied, and if such judgements influence how they will choose to spend their money, then businesses must react. Simply in terms of the interests of shareholders and profitability, aside from other aspects which may also enter the equation, they have to take account of such views and expectations, weigh them carefully, and decide how best to respond. This is not in dispute, nor is it new. But it does not take matters very far, since it leaves open issues concerning the nature, the claims to representative status, and the validity of different expectations.

Such issues are largely passed over by CSR advocates, both within business and outside. They treat 'society's expectations' as homogeneous, given, known and legitimate, and take it for granted that corporations now have little choice but to meet them by taking the path of CSR. Both these assumptions, however, are open to question.

To begin with, not all public expectations, and demands arising from them, are well founded, reasonable or realistic. It has to be asked how far they are based on a true understanding of the facts of the situation and what companies can properly and sensibly be expected to do. Further, the consequences of meeting them, including possible adverse effects on enterprise performance, have to be taken into account. To act in accordance with 'society's expectations', even if these are correctly read, may not be in the public interest.

When expectations and demands appear to them as unreasonable or unwarranted, businesses clearly have a right and arguably a duty to argue the case against them, to stand up for what they see as the truth. This aspect is scarcely mentioned in the writings on CSR. Occasionally one can find some recognition of the issue, as for example when Philip Watts of Shell, in his contribution to a set of essays (Mitchell, 1998: 31), rightly says that companies cannot be 'social activists'. But in general the advocates of CSR are disposed only to stress, and to accept without argument, the case for compliance. One might question whether this is responsible behaviour.

A related point is that expectations are formed, and demands made, by different elements within 'society', comprising a highly varied collection of people, groups and institutions. Among these, the most radical and insistent, and often the best organised, are the NGOs, and it is partly in response to them that many companies and business organisations have not only yielded ground but also developed this new corporate philosophy. But with few exceptions these NGOs are hostile to, or highly critical of, MNEs, capitalism, freedom of cross-border trade and capital flows, and the idea of a market economy. One might expect, and indeed hope, that the business community would effectively contest such anti-business views. But in CSR circles at any rate, the emphasis is on concessions and accommodation.

The strategy of accommodation

One aspect of this is a general failure to engage in argument. International business today appears unable or reluctant to defend itself against unjustified criticisms and attacks: non-resistance has become the order of the day. A recent instance was the episode of the ill-fated Multilateral Agreement on Investment (MAI). The proposed Agreement was subjected in 1997/98 to a strong and well-organised hostile campaign by NGOs across the world, who co-ordinated their efforts through the Internet. Many of the arguments thus brought to bear were based on the misguided view that the Agreement was chiefly designed to benefit MNEs, and would confer on them dangerous new powers; and many of the opponents took the opportunity to voice again their general hostility to international business. Looking back on the affair, after the MAI had been killed off – by the governments of OECD member countries for their own reasons, rather than by the NGOs' campaign – I noted that:

> A feature of the MAI debate was that the opposition made
> virtually all the running ... Despite their many weaknesses
> and exaggerations, the hostile arguments of NGOs and
> other opponents were not forcefully countered. Neither
> OECD member governments nor the Organisation itself

> have made effective rejoinders, *nor have the multinationals*
> *and the organisations that speak for them.* (Henderson, 1999:
> 47, italics now added)

Such passivity and lack of enterprise seem to have become characteristic of international business. In none of the business-related documents cited here, whether originating in the business world or outside it, is there an informed and well-argued defence of the MNEs against the often extravagant charges brought against them.

Non-resistance sometimes goes with a readiness to don sackcloth and ashes, by confessing the presumed sins of businesses. Thus in WBC1999 there is a reference (p. 6) to 'disillusionment with the excesses of capitalism' in its earlier phases, the 'excesses' (though unspecified) being taken for granted. Again, Sir John Browne, in a lecture given in Oxford in 1998, said that

> We start from a position where many people instinctively
> distrust companies and what they say. *That distrust arises*
> *from the errors we've all made in the past, and it is reinforced by*
> *every failure* . . . (italics mine)

There is of course ample evidence not merely of 'distrust' of MNEs, but also, and still more, of unrelenting and unwarranted hostility to them. It is a mystery why Sir John should have been so ready to concede that when people are critical of companies their concerns are well founded, simply because of unnamed 'errors', and should fail to make the point that 'instinctive distrust' is not a reasonable attitude.

A common form of today's misplaced apologetics, which is used to underpin the case for CSR, is the notion of a 'licence to operate' which companies are said now to require, in the sense of an informal consent or tolerance on the part of 'society' which has to

be earned by actions that go well beyond meeting legal requirements. For example, WBC1999 bows twice on one page (p. 9) to
the view that companies have been accorded special privileges
which require, by way of recompense to the rest of 'society', new
and improved modes of conduct:

> Current shifts in societal expectations are strongly towards
> business demonstrating that it can behave ethically and
> responsibly in return for *the freedoms and opportunities that*
> *society bestows on it* ... The idea of consulting stakeholders
> can be seen as a tool to understand complexity and
> prioritize actions. It also reminds the corporation of the
> social and environmental obligations which come with the
> freedoms society bestows on companies. (italics mine)

Again, Chad Holliday of Dupont said, in the speech already
quoted, that 'At DuPont, we ... believe that the primary reason
civil society allows us to operate and grow is because of the value
we bring through our products and services.'

This notion has now been given an international dimension
also. Thus Björn Stigson, the President of the WBCSD, refers in
the Council's Annual Review for 1999 (p. 4) to 'business's long-
term licence to operate'; and he says that to retain this, business
now has to 'demonstrate that the economic growth which globalisation has fuelled confers benefits which *all* can share'. In a similar
vein, the BLI Report, *For an Entrepreneurial and Inclusive Europe*, asserts (p. 8) that companies are now 'expected – in return for the
greater freedom and benefits conferred by globalisation – to accept broader responsibilities for managing their impact on the societies in which they operate'. This latter thought is also to be
found, clothed in much the same words, in *The Social Responsibility of Transnational Corporations*, a recent publication from the

United Nations Conference on Trade and Developments (UNCTAD). Here the notion is held out (p. 20) of a 'global social contract', under which MNEs will take on 'expanded responsibilities' for managing globalisation.

In these and many similar statements, the notion of a 'licence to operate' is no more than an invention of the authors. As to domestic aspects, the nature of the supposed 'freedoms', 'opportunities' and 'benefits' conferred on businesses is left vague, nor is there any serious attempt to show why they might be supposed to give rise to costs to 'society', rather than gains, and hence to provide grounds for compensation. It is not explained how or why 'society' should ever have made a gratuitous 'bestowal', or 'conferral', for which it is now demanding its just return. The obvious point is not made that corporations and company law, including the so-called 'privilege' of limited liability, can best be viewed as a set of highly convenient arrangements from which everyone stands to benefit, the more so now that shareholding by ordinary people, whether direct or indirect through pension funds, has become so widespread. When it comes to developments on the international scene, the idea that recent 'globalisation' has brought gains uniquely or disproportionately to MNEs is unsupported by argument or evidence, and is in fact quite false. (Even if there were something in it, the final beneficiaries would not be MNEs as such. Rather, they would be the many owners of these firms, and also the governments – and hence their citizens – that gained from higher revenues from the company taxes that the firms would then pay.) Last, in all these arguments, as generally in CSR-related publications, no account is taken of the possibility that 'societal expectations' might be unjustified or open to question.

Many businesses and business organisations, in dealing with

critics, have chosen a path of appeasement. One aspect of this is diplomatic silence or reticence. NGOs are consistently treated with an uncritical politeness that amounts to deference. In most of the business and business-related publications cited here, there is virtually no hint or suggestion that opinions advanced by NGOs might be open to question, ill informed, misleading or false. A related form of appeasement is to be seen in the hyper-diplomatic language in which CSR-minded firms and organisations refer to, and argue for, greater participation in company affairs by stakeholders, including NGOs. Public statements ignore or play down the possibility that this could present problems for the efficient conduct of business. Stakeholders, like NGOs, are to be viewed only through rose-coloured spectacles. Here again, the element of candour is missing.

Much of this can be defended, or at least explained, as being prudential language and conduct, calculated to serve the interests of profitability in today's hostile world. There are obvious tactical arguments for adopting a strategy of accommodation. One is that many governments are themselves handling NGOs in much the same deferential way, so that business cannot count on official backing if it takes a franker or more combative approach. Second, there is the point that any one corporation which gives conspicuous offence, by taking such an approach on its own, may expose itself to damaging attacks and hence to loss of profits. In each particular case, therefore, appeasement may appear as no more than common prudence. Again, there is the wish to establish good working relationships, and to strike deals when there is scope for this, with those NGOs that are seen as moderate, responsible, and ready to see the business point of view and engage in serious discussion. It is hoped that this will serve to isolate the NGOs that are irredeemably hostile to companies, and so to weaken their influence.

Questioning the strategy

All the same, how far accommodation is necessary for higher long-run profitability is more debatable than its advocates assume: there are grounds for questioning the inevitability, and indeed the validity, of the CSR-related strategy of non-resistance, gratuitous apologetics and appeasement. Granted that businesses have to react to outside concerns, pressures and demands as to their aims and conduct, it does not necessarily follow that their reaction now has to take this particular form. It is in fact doubtful whether what the public opinion of today expects or wants from companies is for them to adopt the programme that CSR lays down.

The point can be illustrated by the case of Shell, which has gone farther than most MNEs towards accepting the new gospel and putting it into effect. As noted above, the company has committed itself to giving effect to the 'triple bottom line', by 'calculating the "net value" which group companies add to the world in a given time frame'. A document on the company website observes that this can be seen as

> ... a particularly ambitious commitment to a multi-year
> process designed to evolve management systems, indicators,
> metrics and targets across a spectrum of economic, social
> and environmental dimensions of business performance.

Such a commitment, however, has nothing to do with what most people, whether critics or not, expect of companies. On the contrary, it is hard to believe that, in embarking on a course of action so esoteric and far reaching, Shell is simply responding to public

73

demand. Rather, it has adopted the programme because its top management has decided on its own account that this is the right path for the company to take.

Admittedly, Shell in this respect may be an unrepresentative case. However, the argument applies more broadly. In WBC1999 the working group of the WBCSD says (p. 9) that 'To optimize the long-term value of the company to its shareholders business needs to ensure that its values are aligned with the consensus in society.' But even aside from the point already made, that businesses have a right and even a duty to try to influence the consensus, rather than just taking it as given, what reason is there to suppose that today's 'consensus in society' embodies the assumptions and doctrines of CSR? *Is it really the case that what the overwhelming body of public opinion now wants and expects from companies is that they should (1) embrace the objective of sustainable development, (2) recognise explicitly that this has three dimensions, economic, environmental and social, and (3) run their affairs, in close conjunction with an array of different 'stakeholders', primarily with a view to meeting specific targets and obligations under each of these heads, even if this results in higher costs and prices for the products and services they are selling?* Unless and until this questionable assumption holds good, each business has a choice. As of now, there is a genuine issue as to how far down the road to CSR a modern international enterprise has to go in order to meet reasonable expectations, to cover its flank against damaging and possibly irresponsible attacks, and to safeguard its reputation so that its markets do not dry up and its customers move elsewhere. While each case is different, and in all of them there is bound to be room for argument, there is no good reason to think that *at present* businesses generally need to adopt the philosophy and recommendations of the WBCSD and its member companies, and of people who share their views.

It can be seen that the supporters of CSR claim to have resolved Samuel Brittan's 'systematic ambiguity'. They argue that the adoption of CSR by a business will in fact make for long-term profitability, so that there is no question of conflict or trade-off. They focus selectively on the reasons for thinking this to be true. But for the time being at least, the claim is dubious. It rests on the twin premises that the doctrine of CSR mirrors 'society's expectations', which are both well articulated and legitimate, and that the extent to which a company meets these expectations will now determine its profitability. As has been seen above, both premises are open to question. In some respects the adoption of CSR will tend to reduce profits, perhaps significantly, while it is not at all clear, *at present*, that even the large MNEs can only avoid serious trouble by being seen to embrace it in full. As long as this is so, the ambiguity remains: ought businesses still to make a commitment to CSR, even when the effects on profitability appear to be in doubt?

Beyond profitability?

This issue is not directly faced in the main CSR documents quoted here, since they assume it away. Even so, they contain some revealing indications, both general and specific, of the way of thinking of their authors and sponsors. These indications bear not only on the aspect of profitability, but also on the purpose and rationale of the business corporation and indeed of capitalism and the market economy.

As to general aspects, WBC1999 offers on its opening page the following reflection:

> Although the rationale for the very existence of business at
> law and in other respects is to generate acceptable returns
> for its shareholders and investors, business and business
> leaders have, over the centuries, made significant
> contributions to the societies of which they form part.

Here the idea of maximising profits is replaced by that of achieving 'acceptable returns', while a business's 'contribution to society' is explicitly – and wrongly – viewed as distinct from its profit-earning activities. It is one thing to say, correctly, that a company's profits may not be a good measure of its net contribution to social welfare.[3] It is quite another to imply that the two are largely unconnected in so far as profits accrue to 'shareholders and investors'. The extent to which the work of a highly successful entrepreneur like Bill Gates has made people better off is not to be identified with his gifts to charity, nor for that matter with what his company has paid in taxes or provided by way of jobs. To reason in this way is to miss the point of a market economy and the key role of profitability as a signalling mechanism and criterion within it.

The same false disjunction, between the commercial aims and activities of a business and its contribution to 'society', is seen in Sir Mark Moody-Stuart's introduction to SR99:

> ... my colleagues and I on the Committee of Managing
> Directors are totally committed to a business strategy that
> generates profits while contributing to the well-being of the
> planet and its people.

---

3   See Part 8 below, especially 'Profits, markets and welfare'.

In this view of the system, profits appear, not so much as an objective or criterion, but rather as the necessary condition for a business to carry out its primary role, and to meet its true responsibilities, by furthering the welfare of 'society' and 'the planet'.

Besides the above general statement, the Shell report just quoted also provides an instance of the same attitude of mind in a specific area of company policy. One of the actions that the company has taken under the heading of 'Sustainable Development: Social' is to institute a programme for promoting diversity, in the now-current sense of that term, among its employees. This has been decided on the grounds that (to quote SR99, p. 14) 'Valuing differences is an integral part of sustainable development, which emphasises social justice as much as it does environmental protection and economic progress.' The text continues:

> Shell's diversity drive is aimed at changing the cultures of
> Shell companies so that they place greater value on the
> richness of differences that employees bring. This is in terms
> of both visible (nationalities, gender, age and physical
> ability) and underlying (education, experience, religious,
> sexual orientation, work styles and ways of thinking and
> communicating) diversity.

True, a proviso then follows to the effect that all this is in the interests of 'better business results', and not 'political correctness'. But it is probable that whoever drafted the sentences just quoted, and whoever approved them for publication, was thinking of 'diversity' as an end in itself, as an element in what they conceive to be 'social justice'. Here, as elsewhere, profitability serves as a rationale, a useful supporting argument, for what is seen as independently desirable.[4]

Such an attitude of mind is characteristic of CSR adherents. Since a privately owned business cannot survive without making profits, and since owners and shareholders have a special status which is still recognised under CSR despite their being viewed within it as only one set of stakeholders among many, the doctrine attaches value to profitability as such. But for many of those who are fully committed to it, this is no more than by the way. Profitability for them is a means, rather than an end or a prima facie measure of a company's success; and the twin related goals of making profits, and meeting the obligations of a company to its owners, are relegated to a largely instrumental status. Profits are no more than one constituent, admittedly a leading one, of the triple bottom line which supposedly provides a truer indication of a firm's contribution to society. The whole notion of what companies stand for, and how they are to be judged, has accordingly to be rethought.

This is a far-reaching conclusion, and possibly no business enterprise has as yet endorsed it in so stark and explicit a form. But it follows directly from what is in fact the point of departure, the central feature, of this whole way of thinking. *The true believers in CSR embrace the doctrine for its own sake*, because they are convinced that this is the way to achieving the fundamental aim of (to quote

4   More recently, Shell have made an appointment to the position of 'vice-president, group global diversity', with responsibility for promoting diversity within all its companies. Arguably, however, the title of such a person should be Vice-President, Global Uniformity, since the apparent aim is to make the composition of the Shell labour force, in each country and at every level, approximate over time to that of the working population as a whole, so that no distinctive group identified as such can be said to be underrepresented. It is not clear why in logic 'social justice' should not require 'the richness of differences' in mental ability, as well as physical, to be exploited.

again the words of WBC2000) 'maximising the long-term contribution of business to society'. They want to redefine the purpose, the *raison d'être*, of business. Their aim is to achieve full 'corporate citizenship'. In pursuit of this, they want to establish a new variant, a new model, of capitalism. They hope and believe that, in the words of a report from the PBLF, 'we are witnessing the beginning of a new way of doing business'.[5]

Seen in this light, the emphasis that believers place on the demands of 'society' takes on a different significance. These demands are viewed with tolerance or approval, even when they are made by people and groups that are hostile to business as such, since they put pressure on companies to take what the CSR advocates have themselves identified, independently of outside pressures and constraints, as the correct path. In relation to today's critics of capitalism, MNEs and the market economy, some at least of the business advocates of CSR are not just appeasers: *they are collaborators in a common cause.* They hold that a universal business commitment to the full doctrine is to be actively sought, since then and only then would firms be serving the true interests of 'the planet and its people'. The more widely this is recognised – by individuals, groups and associations of all kinds, governments, and companies themselves – the better. In so far as recognition grows, public expectations of business will be shaped accordingly. As a result, the pressures on non-complying businesses, and the risks to their reputations, will intensify. The profitability and even the survival of companies will increasingly depend on their making an open, genuine and unqualified commitment to CSR and corporate

---

5   This and later PBLF quotations are taken from the Executive Summary of its report, *Business as Partners in Development*. The phrase quoted here is from the back cover of this document.

citizenship. Once the doctrine has gained general public awareness and support, no business of any size will be able to stand
aside, and CSR will become a universal set of corporate norms.
Such is the vision which inspires those who embrace it in full.

It was with this thought in mind that, in the previous argument, I twice inserted the words *at present*. Its adherents claim that
the adoption of CSR 'holds the key to long-term business success'.
As of now, this is probably an overstatement for all businesses,
and false for most of them. But the situation could alter, so that the
claim increasingly became valid, in so far as public opinion in general moved farther, so as to take on the character that it is wrongly
said to have acquired already. The true believers, both within the
business community and outside it, want such a change to come
about.

In the new world thus envisaged, the conjunction of CSR and
profitability would be complete. Profits would at last be rendered
acceptable, since they could be seen by all as enabling business to
make its full contribution to society and the planet. The interests
of shareholders would be aligned with the perceived wellbeing of
humanity and the natural environment. Corporate citizenship
would be given full expression. Samuel Brittan's ambiguity would
be finally resolved. Capitalism would have acquired a human face.

Admittedly, all this represents one line of thinking, one school
of thought, within the business world of today. Even among the
large multinational firms, it is not clear in how many cases a conscious and genuine commitment to CSR has been made or is in
prospect. There are differences of practice as between firms, and
no doubt there are many differences of view within them that are
largely unseen by outsiders. In assessing trends, much has to depend on how one interprets publicly available documents and in-

formation. My own assessment, however, for which further evidence is provided below, is that the recent trend of thinking in the business world has been towards the radical doctrine and approach just outlined. Such a tendency is indeed to be expected, since it is to be found in many other places: what is happening in many corporations, as also in many business-related organisations, forms part of, and is strongly influenced by, a much broader movement of opinion. It is against this extended background that the doctrine of CSR has to be viewed and judged.

5 GLOBAL SALVATIONISM: A SHARED VISION

What is it which has persuaded the believers in CSR to adopt such a radical stance? Why do so many business persons, business corporations, business organisations and business-related commentators now take the view that capitalism needs to be remodelled and the role and purpose of corporations redefined? In part, of course, this is a response to the criticisms and attacks from NGOs and others. But as already noted, the business reaction cannot be interpreted as just a shrewdly calculated and hard-headed response to 'society's expectations'. It is not clear that these expectations actually extend to the adoption of CSR; and in any case, the believers, so far from being merely watchful and detached observers of a powerful current of opinion, are themselves eagerly swimming with it. They are concerned to influence ideas, views and expectations, by actively campaigning for their cause. They are trying to make converts. It is this element of unforced enthusiasm, of conviction, which has to be explained.

One possible influence is the development of 'stakeholder theory'. But while it is true, as seen above, that CSR gives a lot of prominence to stakeholders, its leading business advocates have not formally endorsed the theory as such and its possibly radical implications for the reform of corporate governance. In any case, the stakeholder approach and the doctrine of CSR are best seen, not in terms of cause and effect, but rather as having a common origin. They form part of the same trend of thinking. Both are linked to a characteristic present-day view of the world, and of current issues and problems. The vision which largely inspires them, but which extends much farther than both, is that of global salvationism.

The ideas that enter into this vision are widely held, and for the most part they come from outside the business world. Adoption of them has brought CSR advocates in business circles into association with a variety of non-business groups and organisations. In effect, there is a salvationist coalition, although as in most coalitions there are many points of difference as well as of agreement, while some of those who embrace the vision are anti-business.

Global salvationism offers both diagnosis and prescription. Much of what it proposes is far from new, but in recent years it has acquired some new elements. In today's most typical versions of it, there are several mutually supporting strands of thought.

Alarmism and drama

One of the main diagnostic strands, which is widespread and not at all new, is *generalised alarmism* about the state of the world and the trend of events. A leading aspect of alarmist thinking, which bears especially on the role and conduct of businesses, is deep *environmental pessimism*. In this, many CSR advocates in corporations and business organisations join forces with environmentalist authors and groups and a wide range of commentators, whose dark assessments and forebodings they share. Here are four instances, all of them bearing seals of approval from business groups or representatives:

- The report of a Scenario Group that was specially established by the WBCSD asserts (p. 6) that 'Economic success has carried with it a heavy burden on the environment and the quality of life – a burden that is increasing ... '[1]
- The PBLF maintains (p. 12) that 'climate change, environmental degradation, loss of biodiversity and declining food and water supplies threaten the ecological carrying capacity of our planet'.
- In the report of the High-Level Advisory Group to the Secretary-General of the OECD, already referred to above, the second sentence of the opening paragraph of the executive summary reads: 'All major global ecosystems are in decline among rapid population growth and continuously rising real incomes and increasing global economic activity.'
- Stuart Hart, then a professor at the University of Michigan, writing in the *Harvard Business Review*, holds that 'Increasingly, the scourges of the late twentieth century – depleted farmland, fisheries, and forests; choking urban pollution; poverty; infectious disease; and migration [*sic*] – are spilling over geopolitical borders. The simple fact is this: in meeting our needs, we are destroying the ability of future generations to meet theirs' (Hart, 1997: 67). The piece from which these words are taken has been placed on a select list of recommended reading by a WBCSD affiliate, the New Zealand Business Council for Sustainable Development. It is

---

1   The quotations here and below from this report are from its 'Summary Brochure'. The quality of this document, which blends alarmism with puerilities, does not speak well for the judgement of the WBCSD group in sponsoring and publishing the report.

described by them as 'a very good article', an evaluation which would certainly not be mine.[2]

It is of course true that concerns over possible environmental dangers, and the ways in which these may be linked to human activities, are widely shared around the world, by governments as well as people. But assessments such as those just quoted express deeper concerns, with far-reaching implications. They place business itself in the dock, as a prime source of the 'economic success' and 'increasing global economic activity' which are said to be carrying with them burdens and threats to the environment and the planet. The very achievements of corporations, the goals to which they are directed, are put in question. In effect, environmental alarmism of this kind implies a huge worldwide market failure, a yawning gap between the profitability of enterprises and the true net value of their operations. This in itself points to the need for a complete rethinking of business goals and practices, a new model of capitalism based on the principle of environmentally sustainable development.

Admittedly, businesses that favour CSR may themselves not subscribe to dubious and highly coloured generalisations of the kind just quoted. Many if not all of them would probably endorse the position taken by Sir John Browne of BP Amoco, in a speech at Hay-on-Wye in 1999, where he described as 'false' the notion that 'the world faces a trade-off between material wealth and environmental poverty'. This, however, has not prevented a large and growing number of MNEs from providing unqualified

---

2   However, it won the McKinsey Award for Best Article in the *Harvard Business Review* for 1997. Professor Hart gets a pat on the back for his work from William Stavropoulos, of Dow Chemical, in the speech quoted earlier.

endorsement and support to organisations which themselves have taken a deeply alarmist view, such as the PBLF, which is the creation of its member firms, and the WBCSD, which is mouthpiece as well as creation. Moreover, in all the CSR-related publications that I draw on here where broad environmental issues are raised, the treatment of these is largely or wholly one sided. In none of these documents is there any reference to the work of the various established authors, among whom the late Julian Simon deserves special mention, who have argued that past and present widely accepted visions of environmental deterioration and disaster, as also of a generally worsening human condition, have little or no basis in fact.[3] There is a strong and consistent bias towards pessimism, drama and overstatement. Businesses subscribing to CSR have both tolerated and encouraged this.

A second and related element, even less novel, might be labelled *international dawnism*. This is the notion that We Stand at the Dawn of a New Era – that the world as a whole, and people and businesses within it, are facing profound, unprecedented and disturbing changes which call for immediate radical adjustments in thinking and practice. Thus the PBLF takes the view (inside back page) that recent developments 'are creating the most fundamental and rapid changes ever experienced on the planet', and refers to 'unprecedented change and uncertainty', in which there is (p. 2) '... a need to develop new ways of thinking and new approaches to governance at every level of society'. According to the authors of

---

3   The main references here are Julian Simon's *The Ultimate Resource 2* and the earlier book that he edited, *The State of Humanity*. A recently published book which conveys a broadly similar message is *Earth Report 2000: Revisiting the True State of the Planet*, edited by Ronald Bailey.

the WBCSD Scenario Group report (p. 13), 'we are at an essentially new moment in human history'. John Elkington, who as noted above is helping Shell to give effect to the 'triple bottom line', holds that 'As we move into the third millennium, we are embarking on a global cultural revolution' (Mitchell, 1998: 33). Many other instances could be cited.

As with generalised alarmism, dawnist presumptions point towards a need for fundamental change, for new and radical 'solutions'. Both elements are sometimes combined in statements from the business world, some of which show a readiness to condemn the present economic system outright. One such instance is quoted, with implicit warm endorsement since it gets a box to itself, in a book by Stephan Schmidheiny of the WBCSD. The book is entitled *Changing Course*, and was published in 1992. The person quoted is Percy Barnevik, who was then CEO and was later chairman of ABB (a firm which, as seen above, is committed to CSR). After a brisk dawnist opening ('This is the moment of truth for Western Europe and the industrialized world'), Barnevik posed the question:

> Will we be able to give hope to all the poor, who for so long
> have been oppressed by an inhuman system and denied
> economic development as well as an acceptable
> environment?

As part of the strange view of economic history to which these words give expression, Barnevik had evidently failed to notice that the system which he thus denounced had performed in recent decades decisively better than its communist rival. It is worth adding that Schmidheiny's book has recently been described by the PBLF as 'groundbreaking'.

The supposed impact of globalisation

To the already established alarmist diagnosis of the world situation a new dimension has recently been added, namely *globalisation* and what are said to be its consequences. Globalisation is often presented as a newly arisen economic tidal wave which has swept over peoples and governments, breaking down borders and creating a worldwide market economy. This dawnist picture is misleading in three respects:

- It is unhistorical, since the trend to closer international economic integration is not at all new.
- It overstates the extent to which closer integration has been taken: even now, substantial restrictions are still in place almost everywhere on both trade and capital flows, while international migration remains strictly controlled.
- It gives too little weight to the role of governments, which have to a considerable extent initiated and controlled the whole process.

Partly as a result of this overdramatised perception, the consequences of globalisation are represented as profound and far reaching, both for the better and – still more – for the worse. It is said, on the one hand, to have created wider opportunities for many, and on the other to have intensified existing sources of concern and given rise to new ones.

Admittedly, this particular brand of alarmism has been explicitly rejected by some representative business organisations. For example, the International Chamber of Commerce 'believes strongly that the global economy is a powerful force for raising living standards across the world', while the OECD's Business and Industry Advisory Committee has likewise taken the view that 'globalisation has increased wealth and raised living standards'. But among the pro-CSR business-related publications that are drawn on here, it is the supposed dark side of globalisation which is chiefly emphasised. Here are some instances:

- Sir John Browne, in the Elliott Lecture which he gave in Oxford in 1998, took the sombre position, unsupported by argument or evidence, that

  ... globalisation produces insecurity and unemployment ... If we want liberalisation to continue, and it is certainly in our interests that it should, we have to attend to its consequences. There may be 200 million unemployed worldwide. I suspect that figure understates the problem

- More recently, in his contribution to the 2000 BBC Reith Lectures, Sir John spoke, even less responsibly, of 'A world where national cultures and *the credibility of institutions of democracy* are challenged by global competitive pressures' (the italics are mine; the nature of the challenge was left unspecified).

- In the WBCSD scenario exercise, the first scenario to be presented, as one possibility to be taken seriously, is one where

  Globalisation and liberalisation of markets along with the pressures of rapid urbanisation have raised the degree of social inequity and unrest to a level that threatens basic survival of both human and environmental ecosystems. (p. 21)

- The PBLF refers (p. 2) to 'today's interdependent world, where problems of poverty, unemployment, inequality, environmental degradation and social disintegration are impacting almost every nation to a lesser or greater degree', and later (p. 4) to 'the increasingly obvious downside of global economic competition'.

- In a recent book entitled *Corporate Citizenship: Successful strategies for responsible companies*, 'wealth disparity' is listed among the 'three dynamics' of 'global connectivity'. Under this heading it is stated (pp. 19–20) (a) that 'the trading blocs of Europe, North America and the Pacific Rim have grown in affluence to the virtual exclusion of other parts of the world', and (b) that 'living standards have become polarized across national boundaries into three groups of overconsumers, sustainers and the impoverished'.[4]

In these passages, as in others of their kind, alarmism is dominant, while no regard is shown for evidence or readily accessible facts.

In the account of globalisation that is now typically presented by advocates of CSR, both in business and outside, two features are especially worth noting. They may be described respectively as *myths of exclusion* and *illusions of power*.

Twin myths of 'exclusion'

Under the first of these headings, a characteristic view is expressed by the PBLF in asserting (p. 2) that 'economic globalisation is creating losers as well as winners, both within nations and between

---

4   The leading author of this work, Malcolm McIntosh, is Director of the Centre for Corporate Citizenship at the Warwick University Business School. No evidence is given for the statements thus made, both of which, so far as they have any clear meaning, are false. There is no 'trading bloc' in the 'Pacific Rim'.

nations', and that 'the winners cannot "win" indefinitely if the losers are excluded from the benefits and potential of the global economy'. The principal losers thus referred to, here and in similar commentaries, are (1) a large number of poor countries, across the world but most notably in Africa and the former USSR, which have lagged behind economically in recent years, and (2) poor people generally, and the unemployed in particular, in the OECD member countries. The term 'exclusion' is widely used in characterising the present situation of these two groups, and terms such as 'marginalised', 'disenfranchised', 'condemned' and 'deprived' are also freely deployed, as though deliberate intent to do harm, on the part of rich countries or rich people or MNEs, has been a significant influence on events. Globalisation is seen as actively contributing to, if not as the origin of, these forms of supposed exclusion. A prominent and widely quoted source here is the *Human Development Report* series, issued by the United Nations Development Programme (UNDP). The main theme of the report for 1999 was that many poor countries have been 'marginalised' as a result of globalisation.[5]

That this whole picture of events is distorted, and the language uncalled for, can best be seen with reference to some specific cases.

The international aspect

The list of poor countries where there has been little or no economic progress in recent years includes North Korea and Cuba. In

---

5   This report is the subject of a review article of mine, entitled 'False Perspective: The UNDP View of the World', recently published in *World Economics*. A later issue of this journal contains a response by Richard Jolly, who until recently was co-ordinator of the *Human Development Report* series.

neither case, however, can 'globalisation' be said to have contributed to failure, since in both economies international transactions have remained heavily restricted as a result of the policies kept in place by their respective communist governments. It would be absurd to suggest that the international system, or MNEs, or capitalism, have in some way operated to exclude or 'marginalise' the people of these countries, or to deprive them of opportunities, when in fact their economic systems have been kept fenced off from the possibility of closer international economic integration, including direct investment by foreign companies. The exclusion has been on the part of the rulers.

Although the unreconstructed communist countries are now isolated cases, the argument applies more generally. There is a long list of developing and transition countries in which the poor economic performance of recent years has likewise to be accounted for mainly with reference to internal influences. In many cases, as in the two just cited, the conduct of economic policies by governments has been a leading factor. In others, problems arising from war, civil disorder or chronic misgovernment have held back progress: Afghanistan, Iraq, Ethiopia, Eritrea, Sierra Leone, Somalia, Sudan, the Democratic Republic of the Congo, Zimbabwe, and some of the countries that formed part of the former Yugoslavia, are among the many present-day instances of this. In none of these cases can the blame for continuing poverty, hardship and underdevelopment be laid at the door of 'globalisation'.

It would in fact be truer to think of globalisation, together with liberalisation both internal and external, as having been clearly positive factors in those developing countries where economic progress has been notable in recent years: China over the period since 1978 is the outstanding instance. As in earlier phases of economic history, there is a well-marked dividing line between those countries that kept or made their economies relatively free and open, with generally positive results, and those that did not.[6] One of the effects of market-oriented economic reform is that reforming countries have been able to benefit from the adoption elsewhere of more liberal trade and investment policies: 'globalisation', on their part and that of others, has widened the opportunities for people and enterprises and contributed to better economic performance.

This evidence is largely disregarded in salvationist presentations, including those to be found in business-related documents. However, the main point is explicitly recognised in one of the Shell reports, where it is rightly stated (SR98, p. 36) that 'Those countries which have not benefited [from globalisation] tend to have adopted policies which discourage trade and investment.' Much the same argument has also been made in a recent speech by the Secretary-General of the United Nations, Kofi Annan. In his address to the United Nations Trade and Development Conference in Bangkok in February 2000, Annan posed the question 'Is globalization an enemy of development?' and gave the answer 'Surely not'. He went on to pose the further question 'How and why is it that such large parts of the world are excluded from the benefits of globalization?' In response to this, he referred first to 'the barriers which industrialized countries still place in the way of exports

6   This is the theme of the successive reports published by the Economic Freedom of the World Project, which cover the period since 1975. While it is true that the East Asian crises of 1997 might be seen as an exception to this generalisation, in that in a number of countries newly freed international capital flows proved then to be a destabilising factor, my own view is that in all the countries affected illiberal policies on the part of the government concerned form part of the explanation for the onset and severity of the crisis.

from developing ones'. But he then identified a second factor, namely

> ... the responsibility of developing countries themselves, and particularly of their leaders. Posterity will judge those leaders, I suggest, above all by what they did to encourage the integration of their countries into the global economy, and to ensure that it would benefit all their people.

In this, the Secretary-General took a more positive and soundly based view than is to be found in the *Human Development Report* series, and in some business-related sources such as those quoted above, which have dwelt on the supposed darker side of globalisation.

'Social exclusion' and the problem of unemployment

Here a prime business-related source is the BLI Report, *For an Entrepreneurial and Inclusive Europe*. The text of the report opens (p. 6) with the statement that 'Europe faces growing problems of social exclusion'. Later the strong assertion is made that 'The unskilled and the semi-skilled are fast becoming not just the unemployed, but the unemployable', and a picture is conjured up of a possible future in which (p. 7) 'a significant proportion of European citizens are excluded from making a living'. This dire situation is attributed to 'three forces: the globalisation of markets, the rise of the knowledge economy, and demographic change'.

As with the parallel argument concerning the marginalisation of poor countries, the report's alarmist vision leaves out of account a number of pertinent and easily accessible facts:

- The estimated unemployment rate for the European Union as

a whole has in fact fallen, steadily though slowly, over the period from 1994, when it was 11 per cent, to 1999, when it was 9.1 per cent. As of December 2000, the OECD Secretariat's projected rates for 2000 and 2001 showed a further fall, to 8.2 per cent and 7.6 per cent respectively.[7]

- Notable reductions in the trend or underlying unemployment rate have been realised in four of the countries concerned – Denmark, Ireland, the Netherlands and the United Kingdom – where governments have taken action to make labour markets freer and more flexible. Failure to move in this direction helps to explain the persistence of high trend rates in some other European countries, including in particular France, Germany, Italy and Greece. These aspects of comparative performance have been systematically analysed over the past several years in a series of publications within the OECD Jobs Study. The BLI Report makes no reference to this work.

- Now, as earlier, there are striking differences in unemployment rates as between different EU countries: for 1999, the rate in Spain was 15.9 per cent, while that in the Netherlands was 3.3 per cent. Such divergences cannot possibly be accounted for in terms of the 'three forces' which the report describes as having given rise to pervasive 'social exclusion'.

- In so far as one can speak of 'exclusion' in this context, it arises chiefly from restrictive labour market policies, introduced and maintained by governments or through agreements involving business and unions, which limit the

---

7   These and other figures quoted here are from *OECD Economic Outlook 68.*

opportunities for freedom of contract. This latter notion finds no place in the report.

The assertions so confidently made in the BLI Report about 'social exclusion' in Europe, though they reflect a view that is now widely held, have little or no basis in reality. Despite the fact that it carries the names of nineteen leading European executives and seventeen outside contributors, and was duly welcomed by the European ministers to whom it was submitted, this is not a responsible document.

Alongside the twin myths of exclusion, a further leading element in current salvationist thinking has strong implications for business; and accordingly, it is often emphasised by the advocates of CSR. This is the mistaken notion that globalisation, by transforming power relations in the modern world, has cast businesses in a new and wider role.

Three illusions of power

The argument here is that, as a result of the recent onset of globalisation and privatisation – for both are brought in – the power to decide and act is passing from the governments of national states to businesses in general and MNEs in particular. Hence (it is maintained) corporations, like it or not, are inevitably acquiring greater freedom of action, new capabilities, and new possibilities for doing good or harm: for this reason alone, they have to take on new and extended responsibilities. In this vein, the BLI Report says (p. 7) that:

> Increasingly, globalisation and the market are placing power in the hands of the private sector. Companies have far more power than previously.

Enlarging on this theme, the President of the WBCSD, Björn Stigson, has said in a recent article that:

> Overall power has shifted away from governments, both nationally and globally. In many parts of the world governments are retreating from their earlier broader role in society and the private sector is being asked to fill the gap … the role of business has been strengthened. (Stigson, 1999: 57)

In SR98, under the heading 'Debating the role of business and government', the reader is told (p. 26) that 'A moral vacuum is appearing as governments everywhere cede authority to business' – the words of Professor Homer Erickson of Miami University. 'The role of government is declining as is the old 70s and 80s agenda of rampant self-interest' [8]

A similar view of events is held by many other commentators, business writers and political scientists. Here are some instances from authors who have made the point specifically in the context of CSR.

- 'As individual countries and empires become less powerful, international business, operating on a twenty-four-hour basis, dominates the global economy' (*Corporate Citizenship: Successful strategies for responsible companies*, p. 10).
- '… the shift in power away from nation-states means that the public in general requires more accountability from other powerful actors, such as business … Who, today, can effectively regulate an oil company active in 160 countries? …

---

8   The author of these surprising assertions seems to be the only outside authority quoted by name in any of the four Shell reports.

> *As governments withdraw from norm-setting activity, a civic
> empty space has been created* into which business seems free to
> flow as it wishes' (Schwartz and Gibb, 1999: 4, 23; italics
> mine).

- '... the nation state itself continues to lose the power to
  decide on the future of its citizens. This power is being
  redistributed not only to regional groupings ... to smaller
  regions ... and to local communities, but also, even more, and
  perhaps more worryingly given their lack of democracy, to the
  larger private corporations themselves' (Hopkins, 1999: 24).

- 'With national sovereignty compromised by international
  flows of capital, labour and products, the multinational
  corporation is seen as the only powerful transnational
  institution on the world's stage. Only the multinational
  corporation can muster the resources to fight poverty,
  illiteracy, malnutrition, illness, and the like' (James P. Walsh,
  Professor of Business Administration at the University of
  Michigan, *Financial Times*, 8 November 1999).

Statements of this kind are often linked to the observation that the
turnover of today's leading MNEs exceeds the GDP of many
national states: the inference is drawn that such a comparison provides evidence of the relative power now at the disposal of companies and many governments.

All this is misleading or untrue. Three main illusions are involved. *Illusion No. 1* relates to the supposed undermining of national sovereignty and waning capacity of governments to
influence events. Here the point can best be made by taking a specific but fully representative example.

New Zealand is a small country, with a population of less

than four million and a GDP which might be put at around one-tenth of 1 per cent of the world total. Its capacity to influence world affairs is slight. Since mid-1984 its economy has been subject to globalisation, in the dual sense (1) that successive governments have reduced barriers to international trade and capital flows and (2) that the relative importance of international transactions in the economy has increased. There are now no exchange controls, and only minor restrictions on inward direct investment or foreign ownership. The scope for foreign ownership has been widened through forms of privatisation that have permitted it. Overseas-based MNEs have become more prominent in the economy, and all major banks are now foreign owned. Import quotas have long since gone, while the few remaining tariffs are low and it is not proposed to raise them. Immigration restrictions aside, the economy is now close to being fully open. During this same period, the former state-owned enterprises have almost all been sold off: privatisation has been extended to telecommunications, power, airlines, railways and some other sectors.

These developments have been far reaching. Nevertheless, they have not eroded the national sovereignty of New Zealand, nor have they done much to restrict the freedom of action of New Zealand governments in anything that matters to them. All the measures listed above were adopted voluntarily and deliberately, and any of them could in principle be reversed: economic policies neither were nor are dictated by outside forces. More broadly, and as in other countries in the world except for those where no effective civil authority exists, the government of New Zealand retains the power to run its own affairs in relation to such matters as defence, foreign policy, constitutional arrangements, the electoral system and voting rights, residence, citizenship, the legal system, cultural concerns, education, public provision for health, pensions and welfare, and the status of the national language or languages. Here as elsewhere, MNEs have neither the wish to be involved with these issues nor the power to influence them significantly, nor indeed can they determine the course of economic policies.

It is not only with respect to this long list of functions and responsibilities that national states largely retain their power to act. There is a more fundamental aspect. Now as in the past, and in countries small, medium sized or large, *it is public authorities, and not private agencies however great their world turnover, which alone are vested with coercive powers*. It is governments, not businesses, which employ and give orders to armed forces and police, and which make laws and levy taxes. The idea that either globalisation – which in any case is not a new phenomenon – or the selling of state-owned enterprises has now brought drastic changes in this situation is absurd.

Nor is this all. So far from withdrawing from their responsibilities and reducing their involvement with the economy, many governments, even while globalisation, privatisation and related measures have been proceeding, have also made significant moves in the opposite direction. New Zealand is a case in point. It is true that privatisation and deregulation of industries – for example, in energy and telecommunications – have gone ahead there, as elsewhere in the world. At the same time, however – and this has also been true of most other OECD member countries – regulation of businesses has become stricter and more pervasive under a number of headings which include environmental provisions, occupational health and safety, and the freedom of firms to hire and fire.

A recent change of government has strengthened this interventionist tendency. Here, as in other countries, there is no question of governments either wishing to shed their responsibilities or of their being forced to do so, while in some areas of policy the recent trend has been for the freedom of action of businesses to be further curtailed.

Illusion No. 2 is that powers supposedly lost or surrendered by governments have passed to corporations, which are therefore in a stronger position to decide the course of events. Apart from anything else, the idea that the MNEs have recently gained power in the world is hard to reconcile with the obvious fact that they have been thrown completely on the defensive by recent criticisms and attacks from NGOs, and have felt obliged to make large concessions to their critics. In this, they present a picture of helplessness and incapacity, rather than overweening might. However, there is a more fundamental aspect. Not only is the argument without foundation, in so far as governments still remain in charge, but what it says about companies is actually the reverse of the truth. The combination of privatisation and external liberalisation has not increased the economic power of businesses in general and MNEs in particular, but *reduced* it.

Two aspects are relevant here. First, privatisation has done away with old-style state monopolies (which themselves were businesses, large-scale and shielded from competitors). Today's private firms in sectors such as energy and telecommunications have less power than their monolithic state-owned predecessors, because they are more constrained by competition. Second, the freeing of international trade and capital flows has widened the scope for new products and new entrants in the national markets of every country where governments have moved in this direction.

This has made it harder for the established businesses based in such economies to exert market power. So far from external liberalisation giving wider scope for MNEs to work their will on hapless people and countries, as is widely alleged or assumed by NGOs and others, including many advocates of CSR, it has made them less secure and more exposed to competition.

The idea that the large MNEs of today have become more powerful than many if not most national states has no basis whatever. Yet it is not challenged, and is indeed implicitly endorsed, by Björn Stigson of the WBCSD, when in the article already quoted he says (pp. 57–8) that 'companies are one of the dominant institutions of our time with the revenues of some exceeding the GDPs of many nations'. Again, the notion was given a respectful airing by Sir John Browne in his 1999 speech at Hay-on-Wye:

> When the 10 largest companies in the world, including BP
> Amoco, each have an annual turnover in excess of the gross
> national product of more than 150 of the 185 members of the
> United Nations ... that perception of corporate power is
> inevitable and understandable. (p. 4)

Instead of explaining why the perception is wrong, and thus contributing to making it less inevitable, Sir John only went on to say, 'I don't feel that we have that much power.' Something is amiss if a company with such a formidably high turnover is unable to provide a speechwriter who can do better than this.[9]

There is here a general point which relates to the nature and exercise of power. Many writers seem to be under the impression that in any given political and economic system, at a particular

---

9   Further, the text shows no awareness that value added, rather than turnover, is
      the relevant measure of a company's size.

point of time, there is a fixed quota or flow of power which has to find an outlet somewhere. If therefore governments are losing power, some other agencies or persons must be acquiring it, even if they have neither the wish nor the intention to do so: such an assumption is made, for example, by Sir John Browne in his recent Arthur Andersen Lecture in Cambridge.[10] Human societies (as it is thought) abhor even a partial power vacuum. This is *Illusion No. 3*. Not only is the assumption unfounded, but it serves to obscure the frequent cases where a diminution or limiting of power, whether exercised by governments or large business enterprises, goes with, and makes possible, an extension of economic freedom. Outcomes are then less subject to the exercise of power, and more responsive to the free choices of people, groups and enterprises with little or no power of their own. The domain of coercion is narrowed.

This is exactly what results from a measure such as privatisation, in so far as it renders the system more open and makes for greater freedom of entry into an industry and a wider range of choice for those who have dealings with it. The recent market-oriented reforms across the world, such as privatisation, deregulation and the freeing of international trade and investment flows, can be seen as a continuation of a long-run historical tendency; for as Hayek has justly said, the evolution of a market order has brought with it, over time, 'the greatest reduction of arbitrary power ever achieved' (Hayek, 1976: 99). Those who are subject to today's characteristic illusions of power, including many if not most supporters of CSR, have completely missed this aspect of reality.

---

10   'If nations and individuals are losing power – someone else must be taking it from them, and the obvious place to point the finger is the corporate sector . . .'

Diagnosis and prescription

The characteristic salvationist vision thus combines generalised alarmism, environmental pessimism, dawnist presumptions, and the twin mistaken beliefs that globalisation has recently conferred new powers and responsibilities on companies while placing large sections of the world's poorest people at risk. Despite its obvious flaws, it now has a wide following across the world. It has come to dominate some influential elements of business opinion, and the thinking of many outside commentators on business issues and international affairs, as expressed in representative documents cited here. It has helped to intensify the outside pressure on businesses, particularly from NGOs but also from other sources which may include governments, to embrace CSR, and it has influenced business executives to think that to do so would be not only prudent but right. One reason why some businesses have moved towards collaboration with their activist critics, as distinct from mere appeasement, is a shared adherence to global salvationist beliefs.

There are degrees and variants of salvationism. In its darkest form, it portrays a world in chronic and deepening crisis. It sees the environment as under imminent and growing threats of various kinds, and inequality, deprivation and social exclusion as increasing almost everywhere, largely as a result of the ways in which now-globalised markets supposedly operate under present rules and conventions. Such a diagnosis calls for radical prescriptions which go well beyond the adoption of CSR by businesses, although this adoption is now typically advocated by those dark salvationists who do not regard capitalism itself as the villain of the piece.

As is clear from some of the evidence just cited, there are dark salvationists to be found in and around the business world of today. But generally speaking, the international businesses and business organisations that have adopted CSR have not taken this line – even though, as has been seen above and will be further emphasised below, some of them have gone a long way towards giving tolerance or even approval to radical views and organisations. More representative of today's business world is a moderate version of salvationism. In this vision, globalisation is seen as having mixed but on balance positive effects. On the one hand, it makes for general world prosperity. On the other, it is perceived as bringing with it problems of greater insecurity and inequality, while leaving global environmental dangers still to be dealt with. As a result, it arouses widespread and understandable opposition despite its positive side. Hence even the moderate salvationists think in terms of a far-reaching programme of global reform, both to cope with environmental dangers and to ensure that the process of globalisation works in a more humane and acceptable way so that its full potential for good can be realised and opposition to it disarmed. To quote a now widely used formula that was taken as a theme for the 1999 World Economic Forum, the world should recognise 'the need to underpin the free market system with a stable and just society'. Globalisation and the market economy have to be given a human face.

For moderate salvationists, both in business and outside, companies now have a central role in such a process. Like the radicals, the moderates hold to the illusion that the liberalisation of recent years, in so far as it has increased the scope and influence of markets, has shifted the power to decide events from governments to multinational enterprises. Hence they believe that the case for CSR has now acquired an international dimension. Corporations generally, and MNEs in particular, are seen as having to shoulder new social responsibilities, not just to 'society', but also to 'the international community'. They must become global corporate citizens. The possible implications of this are considered in Part 6, which examines more broadly the consequences that might arise from the general reorientation of business thinking and practice that would go with the pursuit of CSR.

6 REDUCING WELFARE:
THE COSTS AND RISKS OF CSR

In Parts 3–5 above, I have given reasons for questioning the case that is currently made for CSR. I have argued that its supporters characteristically link it to notions of 'sustainable development' which, though taken as well defined and fully agreed, are in fact neither of these; that they say little about the higher costs and loss of revenues to firms that it might entail; that they overstate the extent to which people in general now expect or demand this specific response from business; that they themselves actually want to go farther than public opinion in general, which they hope will come into line with them, because – in some cases through having failed to understand the rationale of a profit-based market economy – they wish to put into effect a new vision, a new model of capitalism; and that this vision goes with, and is often largely based on, a view of recent history and current world issues that is highly dubious in some respects and plainly wrong in others. All these are grounds for scepticism, unbelief, and at least partial rejection. In themselves, however, they do not show that the adoption of CSR by corporations would on balance do much harm. Here I give reasons for thinking that harm will probably be the result. I begin with individual firms, go on to consider businesses in general with reference to both national and international aspects, and comment on some questionable political assumptions that often enter into CSR. I conclude by noting the ways in which competition may be restricted as a result of actions, both official and unofficial, that are designed to ensure general conformity to CSR.

The conduct and performance of enterprises

As to firms, the starting point is the argument at the beginning of Part 4 above, that one highly probable effect of embracing CSR is to raise the costs of doing business – or, more broadly, to impair enterprise performance. First, managing a company is made into a more complex and difficult task through the adoption of wider goals, more elaborate internal procedures, and new forms of outside consultation and involvement. 'Stakeholder engagement' and 'implementing the triple bottom line' could both prove costly exercises. Second, the institution of more restrictive rules of operation, and of self-chosen environmental and 'social' standards more exacting than those that are legally required, will in itself tend to push up costs and reduce revenues, as also to point towards lower-yielding investments.

As noted in Part 4, it does not follow that *profitability* will suffer from these adverse influences. Supporters of CSR argue that failing to adopt it may be damaging, or even fatal, for a firm's reputation and standing – with consumers, governments and its own employees – and hence for its earning power: taking the path of CSR could well prove to be on balance a paying proposition. But even where this is true, *the adverse effects on performance remain*. They make people in general worse off, even if enterprise profitability is maintained or increased.

By way of illustration, suppose that because of strong pressures from public opinion particular firms decide to commit themselves never under any circumstances to dismiss an employee, and that they have good reason to believe that, if they failed to act in this way, their sales and profits would suffer badly through hostile campaigns. Their actions would then be in defence of profits; and indeed, provided that they could pass on the associated cost increases, profitability might be no lower after they had acted than it was in the original situation before the pressures were applied. They could also argue, if they wanted to, that they were achieving better results in terms of the 'social' aspect of the 'triple bottom line'. But enterprise performance would suffer, with the effects being felt by their customers.[1] Again, the same would be true if firms followed the recommendations of the WBCSD, as quoted above at the close of Part 3, to institute systematic procedures for involving 'stakeholders' more closely in their decisions and operations, and to introduce more elaborate accounting and reporting systems.

More generally, it can be said that, in so far as the purpose of changes made by enterprises in the name of CSR is to disarm criticism – whether current or anticipated, internal or external, reasonable or unreasonable – rather than to improve performance, such risks are bound to be present. Even if profits are safeguarded, the likely total effect is to make people in general worse off. Both the 'environmental' and the 'social' goals which typically enter into CSR carry with them dangers of this kind.

One source of such dangers is the tendency to identify good performance with the achievement of 'higher' standards defined with reference to physical indicators. On the environmental side, a

---

1   Of course, privately owned firms may choose, voluntarily and independently of outside pressures, to offer contracts which provide for lifetime employment. Even here, however, there may be exceptions – for example, for dereliction of duty or misconduct.

leading instance is the pursuit of 'eco-efficiency'. This has been taken up by many firms and business organisations, often with the approval of governments. In the OECD, for example, there is now a work programme on the subject, in which the WBCSD is a participant alongside delegates from the environmental ministries of member governments. In an OECD report of 1998 entitled *Eco-efficiency*, reference is made (p. 9) to the WBCSD 'criteria for eco-efficiency', listed as

- Minimise the material intensity of goods and services
- Minimise the energy intensity of goods and services
- Minimise toxic dispersion
- Enhance material recyclability
- Maximise the use of renewable resources
- Extend product durability
- Increase the service intensity of goods and services

These precepts are offered as self-evident. In fact, however, they are all open to doubt, when it comes to specific ways of giving them effect, because they are stated without reference to costs and gains at the margin. The issue of trade-offs is ignored. A telling specific illustration of this general point is to be found in one of the Shell reports (SR98, p. 11), which notes correctly that 'Further decreases in pollutants may involve extremely high costs but only a small improvement in air quality.' All the goals listed above carry with them a similar risk. All of them could be pursued in ways that would do more harm than good, and the only test of this is by bringing in prices and valuations of some kind. Otherwise, as Norman Barry has noted (Barry, 1999: 75), such an approach may involve 'the deliberate direction of economic activity into predetermined environmental goals'. In so far as firms decide to act in this way of their own accord, by setting physical targets that are treated as ends in themselves, economic welfare is liable to suffer. The same may be true of targets that are set with 'social' objectives in mind: more of this below.

Norms, standards and regulations

In adopting specific environmental and social targets, businesses are demonstrating their willingness to observe high standards. They make a virtue of the fact that these go beyond what is legally required. In this, they are siding with, and responding to, a general consensus. In the debate on these issues it is widely taken for granted by participants everywhere, both within the business world and outside it, that defining and enforcing 'higher' standards must mark a forward step. For many, such a programme forms the core of sustainable development. Progress is seen in terms of norms and regulations that are made both ever tighter and increasingly binding on all.

Both aspects are open to challenge. There is of course a place for regulation of economic behaviour; and it is arguable, though not to be taken for granted, that continued economic growth and globalisation have brought with them a need for new or expanded forms of it.[2] But neither the greater stringency of norms and standards nor their wider diffusion necessarily represents an improvement. On the contrary, both are liable to give rise to reductions in welfare that may be substantial.

---

2   It is also arguable that the superiority of market processes over central direction becomes more pronounced as the market grows larger and more complex.

Within national boundaries, the history of environmental legislation and energy policies provides many examples of new or stricter regulations for which the resulting costs have exceeded the benefits. As to labour standards, a good recent illustration is to be found in France. The introduction there of a statutory 35-hour week will almost certainly have damaging effects on balance, and the damage would have been greater if the figure had been fixed at 34 hours.

To insist on the same standards everywhere and in every sphere is likewise calculated to make people in general worse off. Countries and regions differ widely in their physical and geographical characteristics, in levels of productivity and income per head, and in the tastes and preferences of their people. Norms, standards and regulations, whether statutory or self-imposed by enterprises, should be allowed to reflect such differences. Insistence on cross-border uniformity may involve heavy costs which bear chiefly on ordinary people.

These considerations find little place in documents relating to CSR. Rather, the emphasis is on the need for enterprises to define and enforce common standards across their operations, even when these are conducted in different locations and countries. Dow Chemical provides an example. Mr Stavropoulos, in a speech of March 2000, laid down that 'Great companies don't have one standard for developed countries – and a lesser one for developing countries. Great companies have one standard.' Again, Shell have adopted a similar approach in relation to environmental norms. In SR99, under the heading of 'Double standards or world standards?', it is stated (p. 11) that

> Our environmental management policy applies globally. We
> have minimum standards on which all Shell companies

> worldwide are expected to improve. These standards are
> high and conform to what is considered best practice in
> countries belonging to the ... OECD.

What is treated here by Shell as a self-evident principle may have damaging effects in practice. Where standards of honesty are concerned, or of compliance with the law, the argument for company-wide uniformity is clear. A strong case can also be made with respect to norms relating to occupational health and safety, though even here there may be room for debate when circumstances are widely different in different places. When it comes to environmental standards, however, it is highly questionable whether and to what extent 'OECD best practice' – even given agreement on how to determine what is 'best' – should be taken as a worldwide norm. The balance between costs and gains at the margin may vary greatly according to local conditions, and the notion of what is best practice should be interpreted in this light.

Eroding economic freedom

It is probably in terms and conditions of employment, and 'human resources' policies generally, that CSR, and related ways of thinking, have the greatest potential for doing harm by leading to the adoption of inappropriate standards and policies. Regulations and codes, whether imposed by public authorities or decided on by big companies or groupings of firms, can reduce economic freedom and deprive people of opportunities.[3]

One of many illustrations of the general point is the official

---

3   The argument that follows draws without specific attribution on my 2000 Wincott Lecture, entitled 'Anti-Liberalism 2000: The Rise of New Millennium Collectivism', which is also used in the concluding section of Part 7 below.

regulations that now govern the labour market in South Africa. According to a recent summary:

> Minimum wages are negotiated between unions and the larger firms in an industry, and then extended to smaller firms in the same industry, whether they were party to the agreement or not ... this creates a lofty barrier to entry for small start-up businesses. Minimum wages are typically set at about twice what the army of unemployed would accept.
>
> On top of this, employers must grant maternity leave, increase overtime rates, raise the proportion of blacks, women and disabled people in managerial jobs, and pay a 'skills levy' which can be reimbursed only if the firm spends money on government-approved training schemes ... When sacking staff or retrenching, bosses must follow long and complex procedures to the letter. A small technical violation of these procedures can lead to awards of up to a year's salary to each employee involved. It is easy for employees to bring complaints before arbitrators, so South Africa's arbitrators have a long and growing backlog.
>
> (*Economist*, 29 July 2000)

One result of all this is to raise the costs of doing business, from which everyone in the community, rich or poor, is liable to be made worse off. But a further and more fundamental concern is that such a regime is anti-liberal, because of the ways in which it violates the principle of freedom of contract – the principle that people should be free to enter into non-coercive bargains and arrangements for mutual gain. Policies of the kind just outlined lead to a wholesale denial of opportunities. Those who suffer most from this typically comprise, as in the South African case, the worst-off members of the labour force.

It is not only government regulations which can produce such effects. In Germany, following reunification, employment opportunities in the eastern *Länder* have been destroyed on a large scale by the phased elimination of wage differences between East and West. This was not imposed by statute, but agreed at national level by business and the trade unions.

On a smaller scale, *the same effects can be created at enterprise level,* through policies that are designed, increasingly in the name of CSR, to give expression to aims such as 'fair employment', 'diversity', 'equal opportunity', 'human rights' or 'social justice'. In so far as all managers down the line, in the pursuit of such goals, are made subject to company-wide specific instructions governing hiring, selection, promotion, dismissals and permitted terms and conditions of employment, freedom of contract is liable to be curtailed. A range of mutually advantageous deals may be precluded. Not only will such enforced uniformity of practices tend to raise enterprise costs, but also, like economy-wide regulations or restrictive agreements of the kind referred to above, it prevents labour markets from functioning freely, and hence deprives ordinary people of opportunities to make themselves better off.

This is not to say that businesses should be prevented from acting in such ways. Among the freedoms that a market economy provides is freedom on the part of a large enterprise to decide for itself, within the limits set by legislation, what its 'human resources' principles and policies should be. The fact remains that policies in this area that are now advocated and put into effect as part of CSR may not only worsen enterprise performance but also erode economic freedom. They reduce welfare by narrowing the scope of markets.

Regulating the world

The most damaging consequences of imposed uniformity arise when it is given an international dimension. It is precisely when the situations in different countries or regions differ widely, in ways that in the absence of regulation would be reflected in market prices, that opportunities for mutually beneficial cross-border trade and investment flows arise. To repress the differences is to destroy such opportunities.

One source of danger here, already mentioned, is the imposition in developing countries of environmental norms which may be over-zealous even in the OECD area, and were in any case not designed with the local situation in mind. Given the influence now exerted by environmental NGOs, and the kinds of commitments that international businesses have made in the name of CSR, there is a risk that companies – alongside some OECD governments, in so far as these are pressing for international regulation – will become the agents of what Deepak Lal has termed 'eco-imperialism' (Lal, 2000).

Just as worrying, if not more so, are the effects of action, whether official or unofficial, to prescribe and enforce 'minimum international labour standards'. This is often linked to the aim of defining and giving effect to an ever-growing list of 'positive' human rights. Like sustainable development, these are both appealing notions. But translating them into practice carries with it the risk that employment opportunities in poor countries will be denied or precluded on what could become a worrying scale.

Recent official moves towards tighter cross-border regulation are to be seen in the Social Chapter of the European Union and in one of the side agreements of the North American Free Trade Agreement. Both the United States and the European Union are now pressing for clauses relating to labour standards to be included in future international agreements relating to trade and direct investment. Here also, however, the risks do not arise from official measures alone. Even without intergovernmental agreements, similar effects can follow from decisions taken on their own account by MNEs. As noted already, businesses are now under strong pressure from public opinion generally, and NGOs in particular, to ensure that terms and conditions of employment, not only in their own operations but also in those of their partners and suppliers, are acceptable. A significant and growing number of MNEs have now made explicit commitments of this kind; and as in the case of self-imposed environmental standards, they are acting in this way not just in response to outside opinion but also in the belief that they are doing the right thing. The adoption and diffusion of acceptable standards are seen as obligations that form part of CSR and global corporate citizenship.

A good instance of this way of thinking is to be found in one of the business-related works already cited. *Corporate Citizenship: Successful strategies for responsible companies* has a commendatory foreword by Alice Tepper Marlin, President of the Council on Economic Priorities in the US. Here she sounds a note of alarm. She writes (p. xi) that 'as assembly and manufacturing jobs move in response to market conditions, children and impoverished adults are hired at rock-bottom wages'. It seems not to have occurred to her, and those who think like her, that the adults who voluntarily seek employment with foreign-connected firms, on terms that they are aware of, do so in the hope and expectation of becoming less impoverished. Likewise, it seems not to have occurred to her and those like her that at the wage levels which they are prepared to approve for others job opportunities may be closed off. Just as unemployed East Germans may be denied the freedom to work except on the terms that prevail in the West, and unemployed South Africans to take jobs that they would like to have at rates below those in industry agreements, so people in poor countries generally, for their own good of course, and in the name of human rights and minimum labour standards, must be denied the possibility of entering into deals with foreign firms (and with the suppliers of such firms) which they believe would make them better off, but which would involve wages condemned as 'rock-bottom' by many European, American and Australasian television viewers, business persons and business writers, trade unionists, NGOs, and commentators and public figures. In such cases, even more than within national borders, those who are deprived of opportunities, through the suppression of freedom of contract, are typically the poor.

These disturbing possibilities often pass unnoticed by commentators on the business scene. Indeed, some of them believe that the interests of people in developing countries will be well served if MNEs practise self-regulation and the bypassing of markets, by imposing standards of their own. For example, Debora Spar, writing in 1998 in *Foreign Affairs*, argues (p. 12) that in these countries 'US multinationals ... may influence the local environment in positive ways'; and this is because they bring with them 'working standards [which] will nearly always be higher than those that prevail in the local developing economy'. A similar thought is voiced by Michael Hopkins in *The Planetary Bargain*, when he refers (p. 36) to 'Raising the living standards of workers round the world through socially responsible policies of enterprises'. For such authors, the key to economic progress in developing countries, and indeed to ending world poverty, is easily found:

big international companies should pay people well.[4] No doubt their works have an honoured place in reading lists for courses in business ethics and corporate social responsibility.

In equating improvements in standards with greater stringency and uniformity, some businesses and business organisations, though they are not alone in this, are resorting to oversimplifed and dubious formulae and opening the way to practices that will reduce welfare. To say that this is now demanded of them by public opinion is not an adequate defence.

A Global Compact

Through deciding and imposing common standards in the name of CSR, international businesses, if they so choose, are able to carve out a role of their own in over-regulating the world. In doing so, they can generally count on support from NGOs and trade unions, and quite possibly from OECD member governments also. There is scope for collaboration here, involving the business world and agencies outside it. A recently launched worldwide co-operative venture to raise standards, in which international businesses have teamed up with other like-minded organisations, is the so-called Global Compact.

The idea of 'a compact for the new century' was launched by the UN Secretary-General at the 1999 World Economic Forum. The stated aim is (to repeat the formula) 'to underpin the free and open market system with stable and just societies'. In his speech at the launching, Kofi Annan proposed that businesses

---

4   Hopkins adds to this a second layer of nonsense, by arguing that if companies act in this way it will provide a 'Keynesian stimulus' to global effective demand which the world stands in need of.

should 'embrace and enact' a set of nine principles. These relate to the observance of human rights, the establishment and upholding of labour standards, and the protection of the environment. They bear an official stamp, since they are derived from declarations and resolutions adopted by governments at various meetings and conferences held over the years under UN auspices. The Secretary-General's proposal found favour, and the Global Compact has come into existence. It has been endorsed by a number of business organisations, including the International Chamber of Commerce, the WBCSD, the PBLF, Business for Social Responsibility, and the European Business Network for Social Cohesion, as also by a growing list of individual firms. The Secretary-General recently announced that Göran Lindahl, former CEO of ABB, will lead a recruitment effort designed to bring corporate membership to one thousand by the year 2002.

Within the Compact, a tripartite working arrangement has been created, by which businesses and business organisations join with UN agencies, and with selected NGOs including trade unions, to define and give content to those aspects of CSR that fall under the agreed nine principles. To quote a senior UN official, Georg Kell, 'A global network of engaging actors has been assembled', while

> A Global Compact Office is currently being established.
> Reporting directly to the Executive Office of the Secretary-
> General, its mission is to leverage authority, catalyze action,
> and ensure optimum synergies. (Kell, 2000: 40)[5]

---

5   Earlier in this text, Mr Kell provided what may qualify as the most adventurous mixed metaphor of the year 2000, by referring to 'the imbalances that are at the root of the backlash [against globalisation]'.

In the process up to now, no specific commitments are involved. As described by Mr Kell and a UN colleague, John Gerard Ruggie,

> The Global Compact is not designed as a code of conduct. Instead, it is meant to serve as a frame of reference and dialogue to stimulate best practices and to bring about convergence in corporate practices around universally shared values. (Kell and Ruggie, 1999: 104)

It will be seen that the Compact is a one-sided affair: within it, only corporations are seen as having obligations. Its purpose is to promote global corporate citizenship.

The Compact forms part of a wider programme to improve 'global governance'. The businesses and business organisations, NGOs and UN agencies that are parties to it share the salvationist perspective, according to which governments have lost power, international businesses have gained it, and the growing power of the NGOs is exerting a new and salutary influence on events. From this reading of the situation, the idea has developed and gained acceptance that the world economy should now increasingly be managed through a 'new tripartism', comprising governments, business and 'civil society', working closely with international agencies within the UN system. The shared objectives of tripartite endeavour would be to make globalised markets work for the benefit of all and to further sustainable development. The Compact forms part of what is seen as a worldwide team effort.

Such a programme of reform rests on the weak foundation of global salvationist doctrine. Contrary to this doctrine, and as noted above, the combination of privatisation and the freeing of cross-border flows of trade and investment has not made for 'marginalisation' or 'exclusion', nor has it brought disproportionate gains to MNEs as such. It has not significantly undermined the powers of governments, and it has made businesses generally more subject to competition. A new pattern of 'global governance' is not required in order to cope with trends that are largely imaginary.[6]

What is more, these specific proposals for reforms in governance embody a further dual misconception. It is presumed that the NGOs can be identified with 'civil society', and that in consequence they have rights to full participation in political processes. Both presumptions are unwarranted. Civil society, properly defined, goes much farther than the NGOs (and businesses too): it comprises all the myriad activities, relationships, agencies and organised groups that fall between individuals and families on the one hand and the apparatus of state on the other. Though the NGOs are part of this, they are far from being the whole, and they have no claim to speak for all. Still less can they be viewed as representing 'global civil society', the very notion of which is in any case open to doubt. Again, no non-governmental organisation – whether representing business enterprises, trade unions or professional bodies, 'public interest' concerns, or any other cause – has a valid claim *in its own right* to full participation in proceedings where the responsibility for outcomes and decisions rests, and has to rest, with the politically accountable governments of national sovereign states. These basic points go largely unrecognised in the statements and writings of CSR supporters and leading UN officials alike.

How seriously the Global Compact is being taken by its participants is hard for an outsider to judge. Since it makes UN

---

6   There may of course be better-founded arguments for new forms of concerted international action today: dealing with problems of climate change, and their possible connection with human activity, is arguably an outstanding example.

agencies appear more important, gives NGOs a more prominent place on the world stage, and offers participating businesses an extra opportunity to acquire credit by demonstrating that they are good corporate citizens, all who have now signed up to it have an interest in backing the idea, inflating its importance, and keeping their reservations hidden. Given that the whole exercise is based on an illusory conception of the relative powers and status of business and governments, it is not to be expected that much will come of it: the element of pretence is dominant. All the same, the Compact has the potential, under two related headings, to do harm.

First, it could well add momentum to the process of defining and enforcing internationally agreed norms and standards in relation to its three areas – human rights, labour and the environment. It thus points the way to closer cross-border regulation of economic activity, whether by governments or on the part of MNEs; and for reasons given above, this would tend to limit economic freedom and reduce welfare. Like global corporate citizenship, the Compact is presented as a way of making capitalism and globalisation acceptable, by giving them both a human face. But the kinds of measures that it points towards would restrict the scope and impair the working of markets.

Second, it reinforces the status and influence of two sets of organisations that wish to see a more regulated world – namely, the NGOs and the UN agencies involved. That MNEs and business organisations have so readily signed up to the Compact is further evidence for the argument made in Part 4 above, that many of the leading business supporters of CSR have gone beyond appeasement of outside critics and have moved into active collaboration with them. On this, a further word is due.

Sleeping with the enemy

I have noted already that the majority of NGOs are hostile to international business, capitalism and the market economy, and that, nevertheless, businesses which have taken the path of CSR typically treat them with a studiously uncritical politeness that amounts to deference. In the international context especially, some business leaders have gone beyond this. International businesses, and those who speak for them, have assigned to the NGOs a role in 'global governance' which does not properly belong to them, and have gone out of their way to commend both the NGOs as such and their present role and influence.

As to the former aspect, the theme of tripartite global governance has been addressed by the WBCSD itself. On the title page of WBC2000, a specially featured headline quotation comes from C. Michael Armstrong, Chairman and CEO of AT&T. It begins: 'AT&T understands the need for a global alliance of business, society and the environment'. (Mr Armstrong here forgot about governments, though this did not prevent the WBCSD from giving special prominence to his views.) Again, Björn Stigson of the WBCSD, in the article already quoted, writes (p. 57) of

> ... a tripolar world consisting of business, governments and
> civil society ... today the issue is how these three poles can
> interact in a constructive way to find solutions to the
> sustainable development challenges ...

Not only is the notion of a 'tripolar world' a figment of Stigson's imagination, but by grouping business and NGOs together with governments he suggests that they now possess equal political legitimacy and authority.[7] Besides being uninformed, this is

---

7   Some CSR authors think in terms of domestic tripartism also. Marsden and Andriof, in the article already quoted, make the curious statement that 'Most

dangerous in what it implies for the political process. As Sir John Browne rightly observed, in his already quoted Oxford address (pp. 13 and 16), 'Companies have no democratic legitimacy ... [while] the NGOs ... have no more democratic legitimacy than we do ...'

As to giving the NGOs unsolicited testimonials, Mr Stigson says in the same article, just after the excerpt quoted above, that 'civil society has matured and is today an integral part in managing society'. Again, Greg Bourne of BP Amoco Australia, in the speech already quoted, referred to the four 'key players' who must work together, in 'a seamless approach', if sustainable development is to be achieved. After listing business, international agencies and governments, he went on to say (p. 8):

> And of course, *contributing hugely*, are the NGOs whose key
> interests lie in the environmental and social spheres –
> groups such as the World Wild Life Fund, Greenpeace,
> Amnesty International, Human Rights Watch and others.
> (italics mine)

Possibly the most remarkable of such bouquets has been bestowed – on NGOs in general, not just those classed as moderates – by Sir Mark Moody-Stuart. In a recent foreword to a publication entitled *Responsible Business*, he has stated on behalf of Shell that:

> ... because we too are concerned at the requirement to
> address those in poverty who are excluded from the benefits
> that many of us share in the global economy, *we share the*
> *objective of the recent demonstrators in Seattle, Davos and*
> *Prague.* (italics mine)

---

societies are made up of three overlapping sectors: government, for-profit business and not-for-profit, non-government organisations (NGOs).'

Given the anti-business views of most NGOs, and the violent conduct of some, international businesses and business organisations might be well advised to question a CSR-inspired strategy of alliance with them; and indeed Sir John Browne's recent Arthur Andersen Lecture, which focused on this relationship, offers a more balanced treatment than the excerpts just quoted. At the same time, a less forthcoming attitude might also be appropriate in relation to the UN agencies with which many businesses and business organisations have chosen to align themselves, in the Global Compact and in other ways. Typically, these agencies too are part of the salvationist consensus, in which the flaws of a market economy are exaggerated and the situation and conduct of MNEs misrepresented. More than the business world, in which many can still be found who do not share the indulgent attitude of CSR supporters, the agencies take an uncritically favourable view of NGOs. This is typified in the following excerpt from the Global Compact website:

> ... NGOs play a key role in both raising public awareness
> and working with business and governments to find
> solutions to human rights, labour and environmental issues
> which involve the private sector.

That the agencies and many of the NGOs should be able to work hand in glove is to be expected, since their views of the world, and the place of business within it, have so much in common. Perhaps before linking arms with Kofi Annan in the Global Compact, some of the firms and business organisations concerned might have raised with him, as one instance among others, the crudely hostile references to MNEs that are to be found in the 1999 *Human Development Report* from the UNDP.[8] They could also have queried the references made, in that report and its press release, to the misleading antithesis of 'people versus profits'.

In their treatment of these political issues, many advocates of CSR in the business world give evidence of a level of understanding no higher than that which they show in relation to the economic aspects already considered. To a blend of do-it-yourself economics and invented economic history they have added a measure of instant political science. In doing so, they have used arguments that are not well founded, and gone out of their way to strengthen the position of organisations which are hostile to business and which, in the case of some at any rate of the NGOs, may represent a threat to order and due process in political life.

Containment or contagion?

How serious the costs of CSR might prove to be is a matter for speculation. Much depends on how many businesses eventually fall into line, and how far they put the full doctrine into practice. Under both headings, there are countervailing influences, some favourable and others unfavourable, so that widely different outcomes are possible.

On the positive side, there are in a market economy built-in defences and corrective mechanisms which will tend to keep the adverse effects within bounds. For one thing, enterprises will no doubt learn from experience how to minimise the costs of CSR-induced changes, and they can hope in time to persuade outside 'stakeholders' to moderate or withdraw demands that would

---

8   The report says of MNEs that 'they are empires – with money, affiliates, subsidiaries and the support of the international system' (p. 96); that they have 'more power than many states' (p. 1); that 'tighter control of innovation in [their] hands ignores the needs of millions' (p. 68); and that 'more and more, the clients of mercenaries are multinational corporations' (p. 45).

prove manifestly costly to meet. Again, watchful profit-oriented shareholders may be ready and able to constrain the freedom of managers to take the path of CSR if this appears to be affecting performance: the recent growth and spread of the shareholder value movement can be seen as reinforcing the likelihood of such outcomes. Behind existing shareholders, moreover, there is the possibility of changes in the ownership of underperforming firms as a result of takeover bids. Competitive pressures may thus limit the extent to which individual managements can act on their own account. Even where managers are able to put the full doctrine into effect, any serious resulting lapses in performance may well bring down corrective action, as in the case of Levi Strauss quoted above: if CSR palpably fails in financial terms, it cannot last. Hence market influences can be expected to operate both to keep down the number of participating companies and to set bounds to the extent, and the adverse effects, of participation.

Alongside such tendencies, however, there are forces acting to promote wider acceptance of CSR and to extend the limits that competition might otherwise impose. 'Ethical' investment funds are one such influence. Again, and as already noted, MNEs are under pressure to make their suppliers, contractors and joint-venture partners meet what are deemed to be acceptable standards: this widens the CSR network. More general influences may also come into play. Suppose, for instance, that some firms in an industry have made a strong and effective commitment to CSR, and that this has pushed up their costs or restricted their opportunities, while others in the industry, their close competitors, have moved less far and have not incurred the same disadvantages. Suppose further that public reactions to this divergence are weaker than those in the first group had expected: customers in general do not switch allegiance as a reward for good corporate citizenship. In such a case the relative position of the first group has worsened. One remedy could be for them to revert to past ways of operating, by retreating from CSR-based commitments. This would exemplify the case just mentioned, where competition sets limits. But an alternative way out would be to try to ensure that the non-conforming firms were brought into line, whether through pressure from public opinion, tighter official regulations, or a mixture of both.

There are two situations in particular where the second course of action may hold out advantages. One is where the firms that have embraced CSR are large and conspicuous, like the leading MNEs, and for this reason more subject to outside pressures, while the non-conformers are typically smaller or more local. The former may then see themselves as having little choice but to comply, whereas the latter can largely escape because of their lower profile. Given the resulting conflict of interests, the big corporations will stand to gain if their smaller competitors are compelled, by one means or another, to adopt what can be portrayed as 'higher' standards. A second case is where the companies favouring CSR have in consequence made substantial investments – for example, in 'environmentally friendly' technologies – which cannot be undone, and which would show a better payoff if they were specially favoured, or if rival methods, processes or products were in some way penalised.

In many situations, these two characteristics go together. It is the MNEs in particular which have been under attack. It is MNEs in particular, in substantial numbers, which have both advertised and demonstrated their readiness to involve stakeholders, adopt self-chosen though widely approved environmental goals, pursue 'social justice' in their dealings with employees and local communities, and persuade or compel their suppliers, contractors and partners to do the same. As a result, some of them appear to have introduced changes, and made commitments, which it would now be difficult or costly to reverse. Those of their rivals that have not taken the same course, comprising non-conforming MNEs and many if not most of the smaller and more local enterprises concerned, can then be depicted as having gained an unfair advantage.

Just such a view of the world is in fact taken in WBC1999, which points (p. 8) to the danger that 'Responsible companies pave the way for others but laggards ride free on such progress.' One way of trying to ensure that 'laggards' do not 'ride free' is through getting public opinion to bring pressure to bear on them and to favour responsible companies. A good instance of such tactics has been given in a recent address by H. M. Morgan, CEO of the Australian-based mining firm WMC Resources. He told of a conversation with the CEO of 'a very large resources-based corporation', who had said to him:

Hugh, don't you understand? My organisation is run by
Greenpeace today, and it is my job to ensure that
Greenpeace is running yours tomorrow.

Such a strategy may appeal to other firms that have taken the path of CSR.

Another and possibly surer remedy may lie in legislation. This possibility is referred to by Sir John Browne in his Oxford address (p. 14), where he says that

Only national governments, individually and collectively,
can set the standards which ensure that those who behave in
ethical and transparent ways are not undercut by those who
don't.

Again, in his BBC Reith Lecture, Sir John said in response to a questioner that 'clearly there has to be a level playing field' and that 'there needs to be something which constrains those that are not prepared to play [the] game, for they will in the end be free loaders on a society that's trying to do something different'. One of the possible constraints would presumably be to make mandatory some of the CSR-related forms of behaviour which companies such as BP Amoco have already chosen, or may soon feel compelled by outside pressures, to adopt.

There is of course a legitimate side to the argument. If and in so far as companies confer a clear public benefit by adopting higher standards, even though this puts up their costs, there is a case for making the standards mandatory for all. The danger, however, is that more questionable practices will be adopted by leading companies, for example in the name of 'eco-efficiency' or 'social justice', partly in response to outside pressures directed specifically towards them, and that such practices too will then be enforced on all, even though this would reduce welfare. As just noted, such actions to impose uniformity are especially a matter of concern if they extend across borders. The combination of 'public interest' campaigns and intergovernmental regulation could well serve to shelter MNEs from their competitors in developing countries who are less directly exposed to the attacks of NGOs and others.

Besides making life harder for the non-conformers both at home and abroad, governments can also, if they choose, make it easier for the companies that have embraced CSR. Such possibilities have not gone unnoticed by the latter. In the BLI Report (p. 8) the brazen suggestion is made that governments could make a positive contribution 'by taking corporate social responsibility into account in awarding contracts'. More traditional forms of assistance could also be sought. For example, companies that are offering 'environmentally friendly' products, or have invested heavily in the development or utilisation of renewable energy sources, stand to gain from tax changes, subsidies or regulations that will raise the rate of return from these activities. There is obvious scope here for lobbying for special treatment in the name of eco-efficiency and sustainable development.

In some or all of these ways, the trend towards adopting CSR may favour actions that will weaken the extent and influence of competition, and strengthen tendencies towards regulation, enforced uniformity and damaging forms of government intervention. This is in fact to be expected. As Roger Kerr has noted:

> The more competitive the environment in which a business
> operates, the less scope it has to indulge in social activities
> that are not strictly instrumental in enhancing its
> profitability or implicitly supported by shareholders willing
> to accept lower returns. (Kerr, 1996)

A corollary is that businesses which have chosen to redefine their concerns and objectives, for example by a commitment to closer stakeholder involvement or to 'meeting the triple bottom line', may as a result have a stronger incentive to ensure that the environment in which they operate is made less competitive.

In so far as such tendencies emerge and influence events, the functioning of a market economy is impaired. The potentially damaging effects of CSR therefore extend to economic systems as a whole, as well as to individual enterprises within them; and as just seen, they are by no means confined within national boundaries. Welfare may be reduced, not only because businesses are compelled to operate less efficiently, but also because new forms of interventionism arising out of the adoption of CSR, including closer regulation, narrow the domain of competition and economic freedom.

7 COMPANIES, COMMITMENT AND COLLECTIVISM

It remains to consider further, in the light of what has been said above, the significance of CSR for individual companies and more generally.

Corporate standards

In one obvious respect, the evidence presented here raises a question about the standards that many leading companies now set and maintain. A striking feature of the continuing debate on corporate social responsibility is the often low calibre of the contributions made by businesses and business organisations in general, and in particular by those that support CSR. What emerges on this front is a picture of inadequacy – one might almost say, of market failure. From the evidence presented here, two main aspects stand out.

First, international business today shows a reluctance or inability to argue a well-constructed and vigorous case for itself against unjustified criticisms and attacks. It has failed to present an informed and effective set of arguments in defence of the market economy and the role of companies within it. In some instances, it is clear that the issues are simply not understood: the executives or organisations concerned are in the same state of innocence as many of their critics.

Second, many large corporations that have come out for CSR, whether directly or through organisations which they have created and continue to finance, have lent support to ideas and beliefs that are dubious or false. On behalf of business, they have been ready to endorse uncritically ill-defined and questionable objectives; to confess imaginary sins; to admit to non-existent privileges, and illusory gains from globalisation, that require justification in the eyes of 'society'; to identify the demands of NGOs with 'society's expectations', and treat them as beyond question; to accept over-dramatised and misleading interpretations of recent world economic trends and their implications for businesses; and in some cases, to condemn outright the economic system of which private business forms an integral part. Substantial numbers of leading corporations and top executives have acted in this way, while some have linked themselves to causes and organisations which are opposed to economic freedom and the market economy. In these respects, the conduct of many MNEs and those who speak for them falls short of acceptable professional standards.

The basis for these observations is to be found in what has already been quoted or referred to above. A final illustration will serve to round off the picture. It is drawn from WBC2000 itself.

As noted already, the report carries on its opening page two specially highlighted quotations. The second of these, comprising remarks by Michael Armstrong of AT&T, was quoted in Part 6 above. The first, presumably chosen as reflecting the deep convictions of WBCSD member firms, comes from a speech by Kofi Annan. It reads as follows:

> We have to choose between a global market driven only by
> calculation of short-term profit, and one which has a human
> face. Between a world which condemns a quarter of the

human race to starvation and squalor, and one which offers
everyone at least a chance of prosperity, in a healthy
environment. Between a selfish free-for-all in which we
ignore the fate of the losers, and a future in which the strong
and successful face their responsibilities, showing global
vision and leadership.

That these glib false antitheses should be formally endorsed, by senior executives representing a large group of prominent international companies, is a commentary on the quality of much present-day business leadership in the sphere of public affairs.

It is not inevitable that the contribution of international business to public debate should be so predominantly inadequate and flawed. Some of the businesses and business executives that are reluctant to align themselves with the cause of CSR could consider joining together to ensure that the issues are treated in a more responsible way. This is not at all a matter of lobbying: there are many business organisations across the world, most of them unmentioned here, that are already performing this function well; and in any case, *what is in question is the general welfare and not the interests of companies as such*. Nor is it a matter of propaganda for laissez-faire and free markets, or of pushing a particular economic or political party line. To the contrary, any such new business-led initiative should be, and be seen to be, neither sectarian nor doctrinaire. What is needed is a flow of timely, readable and well-informed publications, statements and presentations of various kinds – some immediately topical and others more general and reflective, and with different blends of analysis, commentary and research – that would promote greater knowledge and awareness of the working of today's market economy and the place of business within it, and better understanding of current issues that bear on businesses. Such a programme does not demand a lavish budget, so that the number of supporting businesses would not have to be large. But any new venture on these lines should be global in its interests and its vision.

True commitment

From the evidence presented here, it is apparent that, for many of the firms that have endorsed it, the concept of CSR appears as much more than a convenient form of words. It is not a pose, nor is it just a reluctant concession to outside critics and pressures. Of course, and rightly, there is a strong element of calculation in the thinking of all these firms, on this as on other issues. The influence of fashion is also to be seen. But the examples and quotations cited here, which could easily have been multiplied, give evidence of genuine and widespread conviction. The business commitment to CSR, where it has been explicitly made, goes well beyond window-dressing and opportunism. Admittedly, these latter elements are often to be seen. But in the wording of many business reports, statements and resolutions that bear on CSR, there are clear signs that the drafting has been undertaken by enthusiasts or even zealots, rather than hard-faced uncommitted calculators.

That there should be this genuine business support is not at all surprising. Both internal and external influences are at work, and they are mutually supporting.

As to the former, there are to be found, especially but not only within large enterprises, well-defined groups of executives, including board members, who are liable to favour policies and courses of action that fit well into the framework of CSR. For instance, it is to be expected that, for professional reasons, the general argument for higher uniform standards will be backed by the managers concerned both with environmental aspects of a firm's operations and with occupational health and safety. Again, the case for policies based on principles of 'diversity' and 'equal opportunity' is now widely accepted by those responsible for the human resources policies of businesses, while the need to keep on the right side of both officialdom and NGOs, and to present a positive image of the company to the outside world, has to remain a constant preoccupation for executives who are in charge of external and government relations, and who are rightly sensitive to criticisms of their firms' conduct. CSR can thus hold out attractions for all of these four groups.

A further and growing element comprises new categories of professionals whose responsibilities and expertise lie in defining and giving effect to CSR. These include board members and executives specifically charged with responsibility for CSR, 'ethics officers', and managers who are responsible for the design and operation of new and more complex accounting and reporting systems installed in the name of 'stakeholder engagement' and 'meeting the triple bottom line'. Last but perhaps not least, many CEOs have a natural wish to make their own distinctive mark on company policies, and visibly committing their firms to CSR may be a way to achieve this. As against these combined internal forces, which march together with the more generalised idealism about to be described, there may be little effective opposition within a typical international business, at any rate unless and until it becomes apparent that CSR is bringing with it commercially damaging consequences. Viewed in this way, the growth and spread of CSR-type thinking in these companies appears as more than just a reaction to outside pressures: it may have a strong basis of willing internal support.

As to more general influences, CSR is in large part an expression, a reflection, of the prevailing climate of opinion, which affects people within companies as well as outside: these are not two separate worlds. Positive and negative ways of thinking reinforce one another. On the one hand, there is general approval for the appealing notion of sustainable development, and for its stated complementary goals of safeguarding the environment, promoting social justice and advancing human rights; and for many, this goes with acceptance of global salvationist ideas. Almost equally widespread, at the same time, is distrust of the profit motive together with a disparaging view of the standards of conduct that currently prevail in private business. The function of prices and profits, as indispensable signalling mechanisms and hence as means of guiding and facilitating a host of continuing individual choices, goes largely unrecognised. Against such a background of ideas, CSR has clear attractions for many people. It holds out the prospect of a new role for companies in society and on the world scene, a role which appears as both more constructive and more honourable than the mere pursuit of wealth for owners and top executives. It is not surprising to learn that the adoption of CSR by firms has been well received by their employees as well as their outside critics. Even company directors and senior managers, whose view of business past and present is naturally more favourable than that of the average person, have responded enthusiastically to the proposal that for the future their firms should accept a new mission and embrace corporate citizenship.

Alternative paths

The idea of such a transformation of business goals and conduct, from narrow private to wider public concerns, is not new. In the past, it was the main single element in the case for taking private businesses into state ownership. Moreover, the now faded arguments for nationalisation have something in common with the case for CSR today, in that they contain two distinct and disparate elements. For some advocates, the rationale of public ownership was that it would improve the working of the market economy. For others, the purpose of nationalisation was to insulate and liberate the industries concerned from market forces. A parallel can be drawn with the campaign for CSR today.

At first sight, this may seem surprising. After all, the case for CSR is often put in terms of ensuring the future of the market economy, by improving its working in ways that will make it acceptable: on the surface, at least, there is no question of repudiating it. However, the far-reaching measures for improvement that are proposed by supporters of CSR bear little relation to long-established ideas on the subject.

Since the days of Adam Smith, it has been widely recognised that a reliable way to make capitalism serve the public interest more effectively, and to enable enterprise profits to become a better indicator of social welfare, is for economies to become more open, market oriented and subject to competition. It is in an open and competitive environment that companies are best able and most strongly motivated to act in ways that will further the general interest – by responding to the demands of their customers, by keeping down costs and prices, and through timely and well-judged innovation. Not only does such an environment make for better enterprise performance, but at the same time, as noted above, it opens up opportunities for ordinary people, including the poorest: prosperity and economic freedom go together. One important aspect of this nexus was well summarised by Martin Wolf in his column in the *Financial Times*. Apropos of the notion that capitalism and the market economy need to be given a human face, he wrote (8 December 1999): '... a dynamic international economy already has a human face. Its humanity derives from the economic opportunities it offers to ordinary people.' Wolf's argument in fact applies more generally, within as well as across political boundaries.

So far as my reading goes, this well-recognised line of thought is rarely found in the writings of CSR supporters.[1] The notion that the domain of competition and economic freedom might be further and progressively widened, and that this would both cause businesses to function better and enlarge opportunities for people in general, plays little part in their thinking. Instead, the working of markets is to be improved through the actions of companies in embracing sustainable development, meeting self-chosen goals and targets in relation to environmental norms and 'social justice', bringing in stakeholders, and playing an active part in 'global governance'. Capitalism has to be born again.

In formulating their radical programme of change, the CSR adherents have taken a position which they do not make explicit and of which they may not be fully aware. *Defending the market economy is identified with making businesses more popular and more respected.* This is to be achieved by meeting 'society's expectations', through making a manifestly genuine commitment to CSR. How this response may affect competition and economic freedom is not directly considered. But for reasons set out in Part 6 above, there are good reasons to expect that both will be impaired, while at the

---

1   In a WBCSD report of 1997, however, 'freer and more open markets' are listed as among the conditions enabling businesses to contribute more effectively to sustainable development.

same time the performance of enterprises will suffer. The likelihood of such an outcome is the greater because the strongest and most effective pressures for change come from organisations that are anti-business and hostile to free markets, while their arguments find support from the enthusiasts and zealots within the business world: these are the views that are attributed to 'society'. It may indeed be true, or eventually become true, that a general adoption of CSR would promote the objective of making MNEs better liked and appreciated, and thus help to keep them alive and profitable in an unfriendly world. But this would come at the cost of accepting false beliefs, yielding to unjustified attacks, and impairing the functioning of the market economy.

New millennium collectivism

Why is it that so many businesses – together with prominent business organisations and what appears to be a dominant majority among writers on business responsibilities, both in business schools and outside – disregard or even reject the idea that the rationale for private business is linked to the case for economic freedom? Three related influences can be seen at work. One is a lack of acquaintance with economic ways of thinking, which in some cases goes with hostility to economics as such. Second is a failure to see the point of a competitive profit-driven economy, as a result of which it seems natural to define business goals in a way that makes profitability a means to higher things rather than a primary objective. Third is the strongly held intuitive notion that market economies, which are taken to be anarchic and amoral, are heavily populated with non-beneficiaries and victims – the deprived, condemned, excluded or marginalised – whose wellbeing depends on collective action, by 'society' or 'the international community', to bring deliverance from above.[2]

These ways of thinking are by no means confined to the business milieu. The ideas that underlie CSR can best be seen as forming part of what I have termed *new millennium collectivism*, in which mistrust and misunderstanding of markets goes with acceptance of global salvationist ideas and a strong intuitive bias towards interventionism. In effect, there is today an informal but wide-ranging alliance of those who share this view of the world and broadly agree on what needs to be done. Besides many businesses and some business organisations, it comprises trade unions, the moderate NGOs, commentators and public figures, including parliamentarians, political leaders and civil servants in a good many government departments, a range of interventionist quangos, and most UN agencies. Along with the more recent elements in global salvationism, CSR is a new variation on a standard collectivist theme.

Rival verdicts

Widely different assessments of CSR are possible. Four rival verdicts might be labelled, in ascending order of approval, as hostile, dismissive, moderately approving, and enthusiastic. The first and last of these, the extremes, have been outlined already: the arguments for CSR, and the reasons for questioning these, have constituted the main subject-matter of this essay. But a word is in order on the two intermediate or qualified assessments.

---

2   The reader may care to note the use of the collectivist first person plural in the quotations given from Percy Barnevik (in Part 5) and Kofi Annan (above). These are typical specimens of a large genre. 'We' are in duty bound to bring deliverance from above, to those who are otherwise condemned to exclusion.

A dismissive or sceptical view is that, while the general adoption of CSR would admittedly be a matter for concern, the significance of this whole recent development has been overblown. The chief grounds for scepticism are (a) that present-day challenges to business and the market economy are no more serious than in the past, (b) that the CSR of today is in fact not new, (c) that it has been endorsed by businesses for tactical reasons only, and (d) that market pressures and common sense will in any case limit its potential to do harm. When it comes to the point, therefore, and despite the prevailing rhetoric, neither the objectives nor the practices of firms will be much changed. On this interpretation, CSR will prove to be no more than a short-lived fad.

I believe that the first three of these reasons for being dismissive are not well founded. First, the pressures of public opinion on businesses generally and MNEs in particular have clearly become more serious in recent years, largely because of the growing power and influence of the NGOs which the sceptics underrate. Many recent and current episodes provide evidence of this. Second, CSR is novel, and newly influential, (1) in the breadth of public support for the general idea of corporate social responsibility, (2) in the radical implications of the doctrine itself, and (3) in the extent to which businesses generally, and MNEs in particular, in many countries and growing numbers, have subscribed to the latter. Whereas previous exercises in corporate social responsibility were largely undertaken by individual companies acting on their own account, CSR has become an international creed and movement. Finally, for many companies the commitment to CSR is a matter not just of tactics and opportunist calculation, but also of conviction.

An alternative in-between verdict, positive though not

strongly committed, is that judicious and well-publicised moves by firms in the direction of CSR are almost unavoidable today, and can be expected to do more good than harm. Like the sceptics, those who take this selectively favourable view, the moderates, are inclined to think that the commitment to CSR by businesses is often more apparent than real. But they consider that the current challenge from NGOs and other critics is not to be ignored or played down, and that, now more than ever, business and business executives have to deal with outside pressures and concerns in a non-dismissive and resourceful way. This applies especially to the MNEs, and among these to firms involved in mining, energy products, pharmaceuticals and other activities that render them chronically exposed to attacks.

The moderates hold that companies must be able to show that they are neither blinkered nor insensitive; that they treat people, including local communities and indigenous groups, in ways that are fair and humane; that their activities are not generating damaging external effects; that they are aware of current concerns about environmental and 'social' issues; and that, where such concerns appear to them well founded, they are ready to contribute, in ways which are both practicable and consistent with their primary purpose and obligations as commercial entities, to the common efforts that are being made to remedy the situation. Failure to act in this way would be hard to defend in public, and would run the risk of loss of reputation and market share. It would therefore be contrary to the interests of their shareholders.

From such an assessment, it is not a long step to forming the view that, in taking deliberate and well-advertised steps along the path of CSR, companies are doing little more than adapting intelligently to a new and more demanding situation. In any case, the moderates, like the sceptics, think that markets will punish those that go too far.

Stated in such general terms, this view of issues and events has much to be said for it. In effect, it points to a positive version of the defensive and business-focused response to pressures that was described above in Part 2. Within such a company strategy, whether or not the language of corporate social responsibility is adopted appears as a matter of tactics rather than principle. Even if the phrase is deployed, it can be separated from the questionable excess baggage that comes with CSR, including intensive stakeholder involvement, the 'triple bottom line', global salvationist assumptions, the preoccupation with deliverance from above, and collaboration with anti-business elements. The term 'corporate social responsibility' then becomes a useful portmanteau description for a well-considered present-day business response to suspicions, pressures and attacks. It is more than a formula, but much less than a blueprint for a new model of capitalism.

Since a strategy of this kind appears to them to be sound, the moderates are tempted to believe that businesses have in fact adopted it. They imagine that, despite some admittedly extravagant language here and there, it represents the path that most companies expressing allegiance to CSR have actually followed. Such an assessment, however, takes too rosy a view of events. It gives too little weight to the many explicit high-level business endorsements of CSR, because it wrongly sees them as not to be taken at face value. Like their dismissive counterparts, the moderates underrate both the influence of the NGOs and the range and depth of genuine commitment to CSR which is now to be found in and around the business world; and both groups fail to appreciate the extent to which many of the enthusiasts and zealots, within business as well as outside it, have embraced radical ideas and causes. Hence they underestimate both the likelihood that CSR will bring substantial changes to the conduct of enterprises and its potential to do harm. At the same time, both moderates and sceptics may overestimate the power of market pressures and incentives to contain the potential damage, because they do not allow sufficiently for the anti-competitive possibilities and tendencies which, as noted above, go with the adoption of CSR, and which could confirm and reinforce the adverse effects on welfare of worsened performance within firms.

CSR is often presented, by moderates and enthusiasts alike, as a sober and judicious response to challenges that have to be met and new developments on the world scene. Such a description does not fit the facts. Many of the alleged new developments have not in fact taken place: they are part of the mythology of global salvationism. Because the myths are largely believed, because the rationale and functioning of a market economy are not well understood, and because of widespread acceptance of the need for deliverance from above, the assessment of current issues and events by many international businesses, and by others in the business milieu, appears as neither judicious nor informed. Appeasement, and the wish to disarm opposition, go together with a large measure of sympathy with, and acceptance of, a collectivist perspective. The views and demands of NGOs and other hostile critics are treated as more soundly based and more representative than they really are. A misleading view of the world is uncritically accepted.

CSR is flawed in its prescription as well as its diagnosis. What it proposes for individual businesses, through 'stakeholder engagement' and giving effect to the 'triple bottom line', would bring far-reaching changes in corporate philosophy and practice, for purposes that are open to question and with worrying implications for the efficient conduct of enterprises. Across economic systems and political boundaries, it would strengthen existing tendencies to regulate transactions, and to limit competition, in ways that would further restrict the opportunities and freedom of choice of people and enterprises. These various effects, both within firms and beyond them, would undermine the market economy and reduce welfare. Despite the attractions of the phrase and the hopes that it appears to offer, the adoption of CSR marks an aberration on the part of the many businesses concerned, and its growing hold on opinion generally is a matter for great concern.

8   NEW DEVELOPMENTS AND
FINAL THOUGHTS

The preceding text dates from May 2001, and was first published in the following month in Wellington, New Zealand, by the New Zealand Business Roundtable. Since then some further developments have taken place in relation to CSR; and at the same time, what I have written has received a number of comments and criticisms. This new concluding chapter takes account of both. It underlines and clarifies a number of points made above, and extends the argument as a whole.

A European initiative

Recent weeks have brought further confirmation of the extent to which the notion of CSR has taken hold, in both official and unofficial circles.

A notable event has been the publication by the European Commission of a consultative document, a 'Green Paper', entitled *Promoting a European framework for Corporate Social Responsibility*. The object of this document is (p. 4) 'to launch a wide debate on how the European Union could promote corporate social responsibility at both the European and international level'. The case for promotion is not argued, since the Commission takes it for granted that if companies follow the path of CSR only good can result. This is because 'Corporate social responsibility is essentially a concept whereby companies decide voluntarily to contribute to a better society and a cleaner environment' (p. 5). At no point in the Green Paper is it recognised either that there might be problems in determining how society and the environment could best be improved, or that courses of action adopted by businesses with this aim in mind might give rise to costs as well as benefits. A few instances may give a flavour of this naïvely sanguine approach.

The Green Paper refers to the need for new and more elaborate procedures and systems.

- Codes of conduct should be applied by companies 'at every level of the organisation and production line', with 'full disclosure of information' and 'training for local management, workers and communities' (p. 15).
- Monitoring, which should involve stakeholders as well as public authorities, trade unions and NGOs, is important to ensure the credibility of codes of conduct' (p. 15).
- Values 'need to be translated into action' (p. 16); and 'This involves practices such as adding a socially [*sic*] or environmental dimension in plans and budgets and evaluating corporate performance in these areas, creating "community advisory committees", carrying out social or environmental audits and setting up continuing education programmes'.
- Companies of more than 1,000 employees are recommended (p. 17) to publish an annual report on employment and working conditions.
- Reference is made (p. 18) to the Commission's 'Communication on sustainable development' to the EU Gothenburg Summit of 2001, which recommends that all publicly quoted companies with at least 500 staff should

'publish a "triple bottom line" in their annual reports to shareholders . . . '

- 'Social and eco labels', which are commended in the Green Paper, 'would require permanent verification' at the workplace (p. 20).
- Companies are enjoined (p. 9) to follow 'responsible recruitment practices, involving in particular non-discrimination practices . . . '

No reference is made to the costs to businesses, and the loss of welfare more generally, that may be associated with such actions. To the contrary, the adoption of CSR is presented (p. 4) as helping the EU 'to become the most competitive and dynamic knowledge-based economy in the world', on the grounds that (p. 6) 'it contributes to a favourable climate towards entrepreneurship'.

The Green Paper notes that codes of conduct on the part of businesses may not be adequate to achieve the objectives that it takes as given: such codes 'are not an alternative to national, European Union and international laws and binding rules [which] ensure minimum standards applicable to all' (p. 14). As to the international aspect, it is explicitly stated (p. 8) that 'In countries where such regulations do not exist, efforts should focus on putting the proper regulatory or legislative framework in place in order to define a level playing field on the basis of which socially responsible practices can be developed.'

The risks of over-regulation, and of imposing over-demanding standards, pass unnoticed here; and in particular, the danger noted above (pp. 116–19), that internationally imposed norms and standards could hold back the development of poor countries, goes unrecognised.

Like some of the companies that I have referred to above, the Commission does not mention the possibility that arguments and pressures for CSR might be mistaken or overdone. There is no breath or hint in the text that the views or conduct of trade unions, NGOs, 'ethical' investment funds, local communities or any other outside 'stakeholders' might in some respects, or on some occasions, be open to question.

The Green Paper ends with a section on 'The consultation process', in which a series of questions for public discussion is set out; but the questions all presume that CSR is to be endorsed and promoted. They relate to specific steps that might be taken along a path of virtue that is viewed as already well identified and mapped out.

In issuing this unimpressive and indeed disturbing document, the Commission is probably right to believe that its unqualified pro-CSR stance will receive general support, both from member governments and more broadly. A presumption of consensus is now understandable. There is today a continuing flow of books, articles, pamphlets, discussion documents, speeches and reports, in virtually all of which the doctrine of CSR is accepted, endorsed, and in many cases taken as beyond dispute. In this current climate of opinion, the idea that anyone might question the whole approach is apt to be greeted with surprise and incredulity. Such a reaction often goes with mistaken presumptions about what is implied by the questioning; and this has been the case with a number of reactions to the present essay.

Three misunderstandings

Contrary to some comments on my argument, I do not maintain

that the current momentum behind CSR comes solely or even predominantly from anti-business NGOs, nor that the sole concern of a business, and of those who own and run it, should be with financial returns, nor that the adoption of CSR will make for lower profits and is for that reason to be condemned.

As to the first aspect, I have indeed emphasised the role and influence of anti-business elements, including many NGOs, and with good cause. But I have clearly said that today's support for CSR, and the pressures for companies to adopt it, also derive from many other sources. Of the 100 or more direct quotations that illustrate my argument, not one is taken from an anti-business NGO. In Part 2 above I refer to the wide, growing and often spontaneous involvement of businesses themselves, as also of consulting firms, business organisations, ethical investment funds, business schools and individual academics, foundations, commentators, international agencies and (not least) national governments, and this theme is further developed and illustrated in the text. In Part 6 (pp. 124–7) I note that some businesses have dwelt on the constructive role of NGOs, from motives which are not just tactical; and in Part 7 (pp. 137–9) I give reasons why it is to be expected that the adoption of CSR will find favour among employees, senior managers and directors of companies. Throughout the text, as in this final chapter, I have stressed the extensive and apparently growing appeal of the doctrine.

As to the second aspect, I do not believe that questions relating to the conduct of private businesses today, and the rules and conventions that bear on it, have simple answers. Now as in the past, there are unresolved issues of corporation law, corporate governance, business ethics, and the relationship between private profitability and the general welfare. Today as always, businesses have moral as well as legal obligations; and these may involve difficult questions of fact, judgement and choice: I state on p. 22 above that 'there are many situations in which managers, and indeed share-holders too, may need to consider what it would be right to do as well as what is both legal and profitable'. Indeed, I later offer some instances of this. I note, for example, that some leading companies and business organisations have failed to respond effectively to damaging but unjustified charges, and have been ready to accom-modate and appease anti-business critics rather than meeting their arguments. I argue that, even if such a strategy is adopted for prudential reasons, it may not be responsible conduct. Again, I make the point that, with few exceptions, international businesses and business organisations have failed to make an informed con-tribution to public debate on the issues considered here. Whatever may be its net effect, if any, on the profitability of the firms con-cerned, such a failure marks a lapse in professional standards.

The third criticism too is misplaced. I have made the point in three separate places in the above text (pp. 58–9, 108 and 142) that *on balance* (since there is a negative aspect always involved) the adoption of CSR may make for higher company profits. Indeed, I note that, as time goes on and if public opinion (including the opinion of employees and governments) increasingly demands it, companies may have little choice but to go down this path.

Such a development is often viewed as bringing benefits all round, as well as to the firms concerned. This is the line taken in a recently published OECD report which 'provides an overview of private initiatives for corporate responsibility'.[1] After outlining the ways in which firms may gain from such voluntary initiatives,

---

1   OECD, *Corporate Responsibility: Private Initiatives and Public Goals*, OECD, Paris, 2001.

the report goes on (p. 10) to state that: 'Societies gain inasmuch as these initiatives reflect business sector attempts to translate external pressures for corporate social responsibility (law, regulation and public opinion) and internal pressures (coming from employees) into concrete business practice.'

This assertion, however, is mistaken. It does not follow that if businesses respond to these internal and external pressures, and safeguard their profits in doing so, 'societies' will gain. For reasons that are set out above, in part at the beginning of Part 4 (pp. 58–63) and more fully in Part 6, I believe that the adoption of CSR would make people in general worse off, and that it could be especially damaging to the economic prospects of poor countries.

'Society's expectations', even if correctly read, should not be treated uncritically. This is not only because of their possible bearing on economic performance, but also because they may be unrealistic or ill founded. For example, today's expectations of business are often linked to the mistaken belief, referred to on pp. 96–102 above, that globalisation has caused power to flow from governments to MNEs, so that a new conception of corporate citizenship is called for. A second and more traditional element in the current demands on businesses, which should likewise be questioned, is suspicion of, or hostility to, markets and profits. On this, a further word is due.

Profits, markets and welfare

In part, the case for CSR rests on a mistaken though widely held conception of how a market economy functions and how its functioning might be improved. In particular, the role and rationale of profits are often misunderstood.

By way of illustration, here is a quotation from a recent issue (March/April 2001) of *World Link*, the journal of the Davos-based World Economic Forum. An article headed 'Lonely at the Top' begins (p. 24): '... chief executives have their work cut out for them. They are expected to deliver consistently to the bottom line, and simultaneously give back to the societies that nurture their business'.

The clear implication here is that meeting the bottom line, by making profits, is to be distinguished from what a business can contribute by way of 'giving back to society'. The same line of thought is to be found in many other places, including the statements quoted on p. 76 above, from the WBCSD and Sir Mark Moody-Stuart of Shell.

Such reasoning forms part of a widely held view of business, and of its role and interests, which can be summarised as follows:

A business has many stakeholders – shareholders, employees, customers, suppliers, local communities, NGOs, governments, society as a whole – whose feelings, opinions and reactions it must take into account, and whose interests and welfare it must consider on both moral and prudential grounds. The profits of businesses, however, accrue to shareholders only. If therefore a business focuses too closely and narrowly on short-term profitability, this means that it is giving virtually exclusive regard to the interests of shareholders, to the neglect of all the other stakeholders. Not only is this likely to go against the wider public interest, but in today's world it also involves failing to meet society's expectations. This failure in turn will lead to loss of reputation, which can bring with it an actual loss of profits and may even threaten the continued survival of a company. Hence focusing on the public good rather than immediate financial returns, and on stakeholders generally rather than shareholders alone, is ultimately in the interests of profitability as well as those of society as a whole. To embrace CSR is to create a 'win-win situation'. Corporate citizenship makes good business sense.

This line of argument is to be found everywhere, not just in the business world, and for many it encapsulates the case for adopting CSR. Yet it rests on a false disjunction between profitability and the interests of society. 'Delivering to the bottom line' is not to be separated from, and contrasted with, contributing to the wellbeing of people in general.

How might one try to estimate the contribution that a business makes to the general welfare over any given period? An obvious answer is: by putting a value on the benefits that arise from its operations, and then subtracting from this the estimated associated costs. Now the benefits to people in general are indicated – not precisely measured, but clearly indicated – by what they are prepared to pay for what it produces and sells – that is by the revenues accruing to the business. On the other side of the balance, the costs to people in general are the value to them of what could have been produced if the resources that the business used had been deployed elsewhere; and a good first approximation to this unknown figure is the actual costs of the business. Profits are the difference between the two flows, revenues minus costs. *Hence they are a prima facie measure of the good that a business is doing for people in general.* That is why they have an essential signalling function in a market economy. That they typically accrue to shareholders is not the point. The argument for treating profits as an indispensable first-approximation measure of an enterprise's contribution to the general welfare has the same force, and the same rationale, when the businesses concerned are publicly owned. For a business enterprise, whether private or public, to concern itself directly and predominantly with profits is not to show undue regard for owners as distinct from 'stakeholders' in general, to slight other worthy objectives, or to allow greed to govern its actions. It means focusing on the most obvious measure of the value *to society* of what that enterprise is doing. The idea that a firm's true or main contribution to 'society' has to arise from other aspects of its motives and conduct, not directly related to the profitability of what it does, derives from a basic misunderstanding.

Of course, this is not the whole story. There are various reasons why profitability may be a dubious or unreliable measure of a business's contribution to the general welfare.

Some of these are often grouped together, by economists in particular, under the general heading of 'market failure'; and one argument for the adoption of CSR is that it offers a means of 'correcting', and thus improving on, the market economy. A thesis of this kind is deployed in the OECD report just quoted, which (p. 20) views 'private voluntary initiatives for corporate responsibility' as complementary to official laws and regulations, in so far as both are directed towards 'the redressing of market failures'.

Such an approach captures one aspect of the problem as it appears today. It was this aspect that I had in mind when referring in Part 1 above (p. 22) to situations where 'shareholders and boards of directors may be willing, and arguably should be willing, to risk or forgo profits at the margin for such causes as ensuring product safety, disclosing possible safety risks, reducing harmful pollution, eschewing bribery, or dealing fairly with other parties, even where no legal obligations are in question'. I went on to say that even in countries which have well-functioning systems of law and government, 'laws and official regulations may lag behind events, and in any case cannot be expected to cover all contingencies'. To this extent arguments based on 'market failure' have some force. But such arguments are of long standing, and they do not provide a basis for redefining the role and functions of businesses today. 'Corporate citizenship', in this restricted sense (by which companies should themselves look for ways to 'internalise externalities'), is neither radical nor new.

By contrast, and as I have noted above, the current doctrine of CSR has far-reaching implications: it goes beyond the standard economists' conception of countering 'market failure'.[2] Many of its advocates, some of them within the business world, view markets as a prime cause of inequality, social exclusion and environmental destruction. Even for those who do not go so far, corporate citizenship implies substantial changes in working assumptions and behaviour, as encapsulated in the notion of the 'triple bottom line'. In particular, the belief that firms should now conduct their affairs with a view to furthering 'social justice' points to actions designed to narrow the scope of markets. Leading instances are the pursuit of 'diversity' within businesses, and enforcing in poorer countries terms of employment that are based not on local market conditions but on the ideas of foreign governments and public opinion as to what is to be viewed as acceptable. Both of these mean overriding or precluding what would otherwise be market-based arrangements.

Not only in this radical way of thinking, but also in the more

---

2   The OECD report lists as sources of market failure 'the presence of market power … externalities, missing markets, asymmetries, public goods, coordination failures …' (p. 20). The report notes that private voluntary initiatives are also directed towards 'redressing broader ethical problems'.

moderate case for CSR, such as is set out in the OECD report and favoured by some businesses, there is a missing dimension. Both groups ignore or play down the case for improving the market economy by enlarging the domain of competition and economic freedom. Profitability becomes a more reliable indicator of a business's contribution to the general welfare in so far as (1) people and enterprises are free to decide what they will buy, sell and invest in, and whom they will work for and deal with, and (2) there is competition between people and enterprises, the extent of which is itself dependent on how far economic agents are free to act. In any actual economic system, today as in the past, it is wrong to think in terms of a choice in public policy between, on the one hand, judicious, enlightened and systematic attempts, both public and private, to correct market failure, and on the other, inertly 'leaving it to the market'. Everywhere there are opportunities for improving economic performance by increasing the scope of markets and making their operation freer. The effect of such actions is to harness businesses decisions and operations more effectively to promoting the general welfare.

The supporters of CSR typically say little or nothing about this aspect. Even those that are not deeply hostile to the market economy are preoccupied with what they see as its weaknesses and limitations, and the consequent need for governments to regulate the world and businesses to embrace corporate citizenship. But it is largely because meeting 'society's expectations' by implementing CSR will reduce the extent of economic freedom, and with it the scope and effectiveness of markets, that it is likely to make people worse off. Profits will then become a worse and not a better guide to the contribution that businesses make to society.

Responsible business behaviour versus CSR

My own view is that businesses should act responsibly, and should be seen to do so. But I do not think that responsible behaviour today need mean, or should mean, endorsing the current doctrine of CSR. To the contrary, it is neither necessary nor wise for corporations to accept, still less to argue

- That the objective of 'sustainable development', and the means to achieving it, are well defined and generally agreed.
- That the contribution that a business directly makes to the welfare of society (or 'the planet') is to be viewed as largely independent of its profitability.
- That 'corporate citizenship', which is now to be endorsed, carries with it an obligation to redefine the goals of businesses, in terms of 'meeting the triple bottom line' and pursuing 'social justice'.
- That new planning, monitoring and review systems should be introduced into businesses to ensure that they meet a range of often questionable environmental and 'social' targets.
- That an array of 'stakeholders' should now be closely and formally involved in the conduct and oversight of businesses.
- That society has conferred on businesses special privileges and benefits, in return for which each of them must obtain from it an informal 'licence to operate', by engaging in good works that are not directly related to profitability.
- That 'society's expectations', which are not to be questioned and which have to be met if businesses are to earn and keep their 'licence to operate', can be largely identified with the current demands made by NGOs, 'ethical' investment funds, and other radical critics of the market economy.

- That grave environmental damage has been done, and is being done, as a result of economic activity in general and the profit-directed operations of companies in particular.
- That recent globalisation has brought with it (1) disproportionate gains to multinational enterprises, (2) 'social exclusion' everywhere, (3) 'marginalisation' of poor countries, and (4) a transfer of the power to act and decide from governments to multinational enterprises, so that the role and responsibilities of these latter now have to be conceived in more ambitious terms.
- That progress within national economies, and in the world as a whole, is to be largely identified with the adoption and enforcement of ever more stringent and more uniform norms and standards, environmental and social, both within and across national frontiers.
- That it has become the duty of businesses to work with governments, moderate NGOs and international agencies, in the name of improved 'global governance' and 'global corporate citizenship', to realise such standards internationally.

In relation to any conception of corporate social responsibility that deserves to be taken seriously, all these lines of thought and action are no more than excess baggage. In so far as they relate to matters of fact, they are dubious or wrong; and where they prescribe duties, or point to specific measures or policies, giving effect to them would do more harm than good. Yet all of them typically form an integral part of CSR as interpreted today.

Now as ever, there are serious issues relating to the conduct and regulation of private business, and to corporate social responsibility in the broad sense of the term. But the current doctrine of CSR, despite its general and growing support, is deeply flawed. It embodies a mistaken view of issues, events and economic relationships, and its general adoption by businesses would reduce welfare and undermine the market economy.

REFERENCES

Annan, Kofi (2000), address to the United Nations Trade and Development Conference, Bangkok, Thailand, February.

Atkinson, Giles, *et al.* (1997), *Measuring Sustainable Development: Macroeconomics and the Environment*, Edward Elgar, Cheltenham.

Bailey, Ronald (ed.) (2000), *Earth Report 2000: Revisiting the True State of the Planet*, McGraw Hill, New York.

Barry, Norman (1999), *Anglo-American Capitalism and the Ethics of Business*, New Zealand Business Roundtable, Wellington, New Zealand.

Beckerman, Wilfred (1996), *Small Is Stupid: Blowing the Whistle on the Greens*, Duckworth, London. Published in the US under the title *Through Green-Colored Glasses*, Cato Institute, Washington, DC.

Bourne, Greg (1999), 'Driving Australian business into the new millennium through a change in corporate thinking', speech to the Triple Bottom Line Conference, Sydney, February.

Brittan, Sir Samuel (1989), 'A Restatement of Economic Liberalism', the 9th Mais Lecture, published by the City University Business School, London.

Brittan, Sir Samuel (1995), *Capitalism with a Human Face*, Edward Elgar, Aldershot.

Browne, Sir John (1998), 'International Relations: The New
Agenda for Business', Elliott Lecture at St Antony's College,
Oxford.

Browne, Sir John (1999a), 'Making Progress', address to the Hay-
on-Wye Festival, May.

Browne, Sir John (1999b), 'Corporate Citizenship', keynote
address for a conference held at Chatham House, London,
November.

Browne, Sir John (2000), 'Business and Sustainable
Development', one of the BBC Reith Lectures.

Browne, Sir John (2001), 'Governance and Responsibility – the
relationship between companies and NGOs. A Progress
Report', Arthur Andersen Lecture, Cambridge University,
March.

Business and Industry Advisory Committee of the OECD (BIAC)
(1998), Statement to the 1998 Meeting of the OECD
Environment Policy Committee at Ministerial Level.

European Business Network for Social Inclusion with the
Copenhagen Centre (2000), *For an Entrepreneurial and
Inclusive Europe*, report delivered to the Lisbon European
Summit.

European Commission (2001), *Promoting a European Framework
for Corporate Social Responsibility*, Brussels.

Financial Times (1999, 2000), *Responsible Investment* guide, London.

Friedman, Milton (1962, 1982), *Capitalism and Freedom*,
University of Chicago Press, Chicago.

Halfon, Robert (1998), *Corporate Irresponsibility: Is business
appeasing anti-business activists?*, Social Affairs Unit, Research
Report 26, London.

Hart, Stuart L. (1997), 'Beyond Greening: Strategies for a

Sustainable World', *Harvard Business Review*, January/ February, pp. 66–76.

Hayek, F. A. (1976), *Law, Legislation and Liberty*, Vol. 2, 'The Mirage of Social Justice', Routledge and Kegan Paul, London.

Henderson, David (1999), *The MAI Affair: A Story and Its Lessons*, Royal Institute of International Affairs, London. (Also published in Melbourne and Wellington, and in Paris in French translation.)

Henderson, David (2000), 'False Perspective: The UNDP View of the World', *World Economics*, Vol. 1, No. 1, January–March.

Henderson, David (2001), *Anti-Liberalism 2000: The Rise of New Millennium Collectivism*, the 30th Wincott Lecture, Institute of Economic Affairs, London.

Holliday, Chad (2000), 'Business Growth and Sustainability – Challenges for the New Century', address delivered in Tokyo, Japan, 23 May.

Hopkins, Michael (1999), *The Planetary Bargain: Corporate Social Responsibility Comes of Age*, Macmillan, London.

International Chamber of Commerce (ICC) (2000), 'The Budapest Business Declaration', May.

Jolly, Richard (2000), 'False Attack: Misrepresenting the Human Development Report', *World Economics*, Vol. 1, No. 3, July–September.

Kell, Georg (2000), 'Remarks on the Global Compact', contribution to a conference on corporate citizenship held at the Royal Institute of International Affairs, London, October.

Kell, Georg & Ruggie, John Gerard (1999), 'Global markets and social legitimacy: the case for the "Global Compact"', *Transnational Corporations*, Vol. 8, No. 3, December.

Kerr, Roger (1996), 'The Meaning of Corporate Social

Responsibility', in *MMP Must Mean Much More Progress*, New Zealand Business Roundtable, Wellington, New Zealand.

Lal, Deepak (2000), 'The New Cultural Imperialism: The Greens and Economic Development', Julian Simon Memorial Lecture, Liberty Institute, Delhi, India.

McIntosh, Malcolm, Leipziger, Deborah, Jones, Keith & Coleman, Gill (1998), *Corporate Citizenship: Successful strategies for responsible companies*, Financial Times Pitman Publishing, London.

Mitchell, John (ed.) (1998), *Companies in a World of Conflict*, Royal Institute of International Affairs and Earthscan, London.

Moody-Stuart, Sir Mark (2000), Foreword to *Responsible Business, Financial Times*, London.

Morgan, H. M. (2000), 'Greenhouse, Sustainability and Industry: An Industry View', address delivered in Australia in November.

Munk, Nina (1999), 'How Levi's Trashed a Great American Brand', *Fortune*, 12 April.

Organisation for Economic Cooperation and Development (1997), *Guiding the Transition to Sustainable Development: A Critical Role for the OECD*, Report of the High-Level Advisory Group on the Environment, OECD, Paris, France.

Organisation for Economic Cooperation and Development (1998), *Eco-efficiency*, OECD, Paris, France.

Organisation for Economic Cooperation and Development (2000a), *The OECD Guidelines for Multinational Enterprises: Revision 2000*, OECD, Paris, France.

Organisation for Economic Cooperation and Development (2000b), *Economic Outlook 68*, OECD, Paris, France, December.

Organisation for Economic Cooperation and Development
(2001), *Corporate Responsibility: Private Initiatives and Public
Goals*, Paris, France.

Prince of Wales Business Leaders Forum (1996), *Business as
Partners in Development* (Executive Summary), London.

Schmidheiny, Stephan, with the Business Council for Sustainable
Development, *Changing Course: A Global Business Perspective
on Development and the Environment*, MIT Press, Cambridge,
MA, USA.

Schwartz, Peter & Gibb, Blair (1999), *When Good Companies Do
Bad Things: Responsibility and Risk in an Age of Globalization*,
Wiley, New York.

Shell International Petroleum Company (1998), *Profits and
Principles – does there have to be a choice?*, the Shell Report,
second edition, London.

Shell International Petroleum Company (1999a), *People, planet
and profits: an act of commitment*, the Shell Report, London.

Shell International Petroleum Company (1999b), *Listening and
Responding: Dialogue with our stakeholders*, London.

Shell International Petroleum Company (2000), *How Do We
Stand? People, planet and profits*, the Shell Report, London.

Shell International Petroleum Company (2001), *People, planet and
profits*, the Shell Report, London.

Simon, Julian L. (ed.) (1995), *The State of Humanity*, Blackwell,
Oxford.

Simon, Julian L. (1996), *The Ultimate Resource 2*, Princeton
University Press, Princeton, NJ, USA.

Spar, Debora L. (1998), 'The Spotlight and the Bottom Line',
Foreign Affairs, Vol. 77, No. 2, March/April, pp. 7–12.

Stavropoulos, William S. (2000a), 'Building a Sustainable

Enterprise: Doing Business in a World with Nowhere to Hide', keynote address at Sustainable Business Forum, March.

Stavropoulos, William S. (2000b), 'On the Road to Sustainable Development', keynote address at Society of Automotive Engineers, October.

Stigson, Björn (1999), 'The New International Agenda for Sustainable Development', *BCA Papers*, Vol. 1, No. 2, September.

United Nations Conference on Trade and Development (1999), *The Social Responsibility of Transnational Corporations*, New York and Geneva.

United Nations Development Programme (1999), *Human Development Report 1999*, United Nations, New York.

World Business Council for Sustainable Development (1998), *Exploring Sustainable Development*, WBCSD Global Scenarios 2000–2050, Summary Brochure, Geneva, Switzerland.

World Business Council for Sustainable Development (1999), *Corporate Social Responsibility*, Geneva, Switzerland.

World Business Council for Sustainable Development (2000), *Corporate Social Responsibility: Making good business sense*, Geneva, Switzerland.

World Commission on Environment and Development (1987), *Our Common Future*, Oxford University Press, Oxford.

ABOUT THE IEA

The Institute is a research and educational charity (No. CC 235 351), limited by guarantee. Its mission is to improve understanding of the fundamental institutions of a free society with particular reference to the role of markets in solving economic and social problems.

The IEA achieves its mission by:

- a high-quality publishing programme
- conferences, seminars, lectures and other events
- outreach to school and college students
- brokering media introductions and appearances

The IEA, which was established in 1955 by the late Sir Antony Fisher, is an educational charity, not a political organisation. It is independent of any political party or group and does not carry on activities intended to affect support for any political party or candidate in any election or referendum, or at any other time. It is financed by sales of publications, conference fees and voluntary donations.

In addition to its main series of publications the IEA also publishes a quarterly journal, *Economic Affairs*, and has two specialist programmes – Environment and Technology, and Education.

The IEA is aided in its work by a distinguished international Academic Advisory Council and an eminent panel of Honorary Fellows. Together with other academics, they review prospective IEA publications, their comments being passed on anonymously to authors. All IEA papers are therefore subject to the same rigorous independent refereeing process as used by leading academic journals.

IEA publications enjoy widespread classroom use and course adoptions in schools and universities. They are also sold throughout the world and often translated/reprinted.

Since 1974 the IEA has helped to create a world-wide network of 100 similar institutions in over 70 countries. They are all independent but share the IEA's mission.

Views expressed in the IEA's publications are those of the authors, not those of the Institute (which has no corporate view), its Managing Trustees, Academic Advisory Council members or senior staff.

Members of the Institute's Academic Advisory Council, Honorary Fellows, Trustees and Staff are listed on the following page.

The Institute gratefully acknowledges financial support for its publications programme and other work from a generous benefaction by the late Alec and Beryl Warren.

For information about subscriptions to IEA publications, please contact:

Subscriptions
The Institute of Economic Affairs
2 Lord North Street
London SW1P 3LB

Tel: 020 7799 8900
Fax: 020 7799 2137
Website: www.iea.org.uk/books/subscribe.htm

Other papers recently published by the IEA include:

WHO, What and Why?
Transnational Government, Legitimacy and the World Health Organization
Roger Scruton
Occasional Paper 113
ISBN 0 255 36487 3

The World Turned Rightside Up
A New Trading Agenda for the Age of Globalisation
John C. Hulsman
Occasional Paper 114
ISBN 0 255 36495 4

The Representation of Business in English Literature
Introduced and edited by Arthur Pollard
Readings 53
ISBN 0 255 36491 1

Anti-Liberalism 2000
The Rise of New Millennium Collectivism
David Henderson
Occasional Paper 115
ISBN 0 255 36497 0

Capitalism, Morality and Markets
Brian Griffiths, Robert A. Sirico, Norman Barry & Frank Field
Readings 54
ISBN 0 255 36496 2

A Conversation with Harris and Seldon
Ralph Harris & Arthur Seldon
Occasional Paper 116
ISBN 0 255 36498 9

Malaria and the DDT Story
Richard Tren & Roger Bate
Occasional Paper 117
ISBN 0 255 36499 7

A Plea to Economists Who Favour Liberty: Assist the Everyman
Daniel B. Klein
Occasional Paper 118
ISBN 0 255 36501 2

Waging the War of Ideas
John Blundell
Occasional Paper 119
ISBN 0 255 36500 4

The Changing Fortunes of Economic Liberalism

Yesterday, Today and Tomorrow
David Henderson
Occasional Paper 105 (new edition)
ISBN 0 255 36520 9

The Global Education Industry

Lessons from Private Education in Developing Countries
James Tooley
Hobart Paper 141 (new edition)
ISBN 0 255 36503 9

Saving Our Streams

*The Role of the Anglers' Conservation Association in
Protecting English and Welsh Rivers*
Roger Bate
Research Monograph 53
ISBN 0 255 36494 6

Better Off Out?

The Benefits or Costs of EU Membership
Brian Hindley & Martin Howe
Occasional Paper 99 (new edition)
ISBN 0 255 36502 0

To order copies of currently available IEA papers, or to enquire about availability, please contact:

Lavis Marketing
73 Lime Walk
Oxford OX3 7AD

Tel: 01865 767575
Fax: 01865 750079
Email: orders@lavismarketing.co.uk